"Now more than ever, Christians need to know how to defend the truth of God's Word in the midst of an increasingly hostile world. In this book for Christians and non-Christians alike, Gilbert sets forth compelling arguments in support of the trustworthiness of the Bible—equipping believers with an important tool for engaging a skeptical world."

**Josh McDowell,** author and speaker

"This book fills a great need in a day when people raise all kinds of legitimate questions about the Bible and its trustworthiness before they'll even open it to take a look. Greg Gilbert's *Why Trust the Bible?* answers that question by examining a series of issues people often raise in order to *not* take a look at this greatest of books. In everyday language, he shows why we can trust Scripture and pay attention to what it says about life."

**Darrell L. Bock,** Executive Director of Cultural Engagement, Howard G. Hendricks Center, and Senior Research Professor of New Testament Studies, Dallas Theological Seminary

"'Can we really trust the Bible?' It's an important question to consider, especially in the face of our culture's skepticism. Greg Gilbert takes on this question directly, providing clear and convincing answers that will help the reader fully trust the Scriptures. *Why Trust the Bible?* is a great resource for equipping Christians to passionately defend the Bible, and it also challenges skeptics to rethink their position. I benefitted greatly from reading this book."

**Christian Wegert,** Senior Pastor, Arche Gemeinde, Hamburg, Germany

"This outstanding book provides a magnificent summary of the evidence in support of the Bible's historicity. It is well argued, brief, thorough, highly readable, and compelling. I not only recommend it but will also seek to give it to many friends—both believers and skeptics."

**William Taylor,** Rector, St. Helen's Bishopsgate, London; author, *Understanding the Times* and *Partnership*

"Many students I meet know that they should trust the Bible, but they don't know why—and so they often don't. This book tackles that question with clarity and ease. Well researched and accessibly written, this will be one of my new go-to resources for earnest seekers and new believers."

**J. D. Greear,** Lead Pastor, The Summit Church, Durham, North Carolina; author, *Jesus, Continued . . . Why the Spirit Inside You Is Better Than Jesus Beside You*

"Greg Gilbert makes for a friendly, convincing guide along one important pathway to trusting the Bible. He lays out an amazingly simple strand of good sense that weaves its way right through the many complex arguments for Scripture's reliability as a historical document. For those investigating the Bible—and for those who love to share it—this book lights the way, not only to clear thinking about Scripture but also to meeting the risen Christ."

**Kathleen B. Nielson,** Director of Women's Initiatives, The Gospel Coalition

Why Trust the Bible?

# Why Trust the
# Bible?

Greg Gilbert

**CROSSWAY**®

WHEATON, ILLINOIS

Cover design: Matthew Wahl

First printing 2015

Printed in the United States of America

Trade paperback ISBN: 978-1-4335-4346-3
ePub ISBN: 978-1-4335-4349-4
PDF ISBN: 978-1-4335-4347-0
Mobipocket ISBN: 978-1-4335-4348-7

**Library of Congress Cataloging-in-Publication Data**

Gilbert, Greg, 1977–
   Why trust the Bible? / Greg Gilbert.
      pages cm.—(9Marks books)
   Includes bibliographical references and index.
   ISBN 978-1-4335-4346-3 (hc)
   1. Bible—Evidences, authority, etc. I. Title.
BS480.G55       2015
220.1—dc23                      2015007181

Crossway is a publishing ministry of Good News Publishers.

| LB | | 30 | 29 | 28 | 27 | 26 | 25 | 24 | 23 | 22 | 21 | 20 |
|----|----|----|----|----|----|----|----|----|----|----|----|----|
| 16 | 15 | 14 | 13 | 12 | 11 | 10 | 9 | 8 | 7 | 6 | 5 | 4 |

To Mom and Dad.
You were the first to teach me that the Bible—
and the Savior it reveals—
are worthy to be trusted.

# Contents

# 1

# Don't Believe Everything You Read

Don't believe everything you read. Everybody knows that.

Especially in our age of the Internet, only a misguided person takes as absolute truth everything he or she reads. From newspapers and magazines to tabloids and click-bait online "news" services, one of the most valuable skills we can learn is telling the difference between fact and fiction, truth and fabrication. We don't want to be dupes, and we're *right* not to want that.

In my own family, my wife and I are trying very hard to teach our children exactly that—the skill of reading and listening carefully, of not accepting everything they read or hear at face value but rather putting it to the test and seeing if it seems trustworthy. Even with our five-year-old daughter, we're working on trying to teach her to recognize the difference between things that are real and things that are "just a story." She's gotten pretty good at it too:

- George Washington was the first president of the United States. "That's real, Dad."

- Uncle Matt got a new job and moved to a different city. "That's real too."
- Batman chased down the Joker and threw him in jail. "No, that's just a story."
- Elsa built an ice castle with her special power of freezing thin air. "Just a story."
- Superman flew into the air? "Story."
- A long time ago, in a galaxy far, far away . . . ? "Story!"

But then imagine I throw her a curveball. A man named Jesus was born to a virgin about two thousand years ago, claimed to be God, did miracles like walking on water and raising people from the dead, was crucified on a Roman cross, and then rose from the dead and ascended into heaven, where he now reigns as King of the universe.

How is she supposed to answer that one? "Um, real?"

If you're a Christian, then I'm sure you'd answer it with a firm "That's real." But let's be honest. Most people in our culture think it very strange for normal, seemingly well-adjusted individuals to take that story seriously. And if they had the chance, they'd probably smile politely and ask, "Okay, but wouldn't it make more sense—wouldn't it be slightly *less ridiculous*—for everyone to admit that those fantastical stories about Jesus are just that—stories? Isn't it just unreasonable to think those stories are meant to be taken seriously, to be thought of as *real*?"

In my experience as a Christian and pastor, it's encouraging to me to see how firmly Christians really do seem to trust the Bible. They believe it, they stake their lives on it, and they try to obey it. When it says something that challenges their beliefs or behavior, they try to submit to it. In short, they allow the Bible to function as the foundation of their lives and faith. For all these hopeful signs, though, my experience also tells me that a good number of Christians can't really explain *why* they trust the Bible. They just do.

Oh, they give lots of reasons. Sometimes they'll say that the Holy Spirit has convinced them of it. Other times they'll suggest that the best evidence for the Bible's truth is its work in their lives or that it simply has "the ring of truth" about it. Some will point to data about how archaeology corroborates some of the Bible's statements. Others, when pressed, will throw up their hands and say, "Well, you just have to accept it on faith."

Now, in their own way, all these points represent legitimate reasons for Christians to trust the Bible, but whatever else we might say about these answers, none of them will likely go very far in convincing someone who *doesn't* yet trust the Bible to *start* trusting it. Quite to the contrary, when a Christian replies to challenges against the Bible with an answer like, "You just have to accept it on faith," the challenger will most likely hear that as confirming all his doubts and walk away declaring victory. *Oh*, he thinks, *there we are. You really don't have any reason at all for believing the Bible. You just . . . do. Because of faith.*

So if you're a Christian, let me put it to you straight: Why do you trust the Bible? How would you explain to someone who doesn't believe the Bible *why* you trust it? By the end of this book, I hope you'll be able to give an answer to that question, not just one that will make you feel good while the other guy is quite sure he has won the argument but rather one that will at least convince him that he needs to think about it a little more. The apostle Peter wrote in 1 Peter 3:15 that we as Christians should "always [be] prepared to make a defense" for the hope that is in us. In our day, that defense has to go all the way to the first question, because long before we even get to questions like *who is Jesus?* or *what is the gospel?*, another question vexes many people around us, a question they want to ask but (if they're honest) doubt we can answer: Why do you trust the Bible in the first place?

## Turtles All the Way Down

Before we go any farther, let me admit something right up front, something that probably won't surprise you in the least. I am a Christian, a sold-out, convinced, everything-your-mother-told-you-to-watch-out-for Christian. I believe the Bible is true, I believe the Red Sea split in half, I believe the walls of Jericho fell down and that Jesus walked on water and healed some people and threw demons out of others. I believe God flooded the world and saved Noah, I believe Jonah was swallowed by a gigantic fish, and I believe Jesus was born of a virgin. And above all, I believe Jesus died and then got up from the dead—not in some spiritual or metaphorical sense but bodily and historically and *for real*. I believe all that.

In fact, there's no use pretending otherwise: The main reason that I believe the Bible is true is precisely because I believe

Jesus was resurrected from the dead. Now whether or not you agree with me about the resurrection, you can probably see why believing that would quickly and strongly lead me to trust the Bible. If Jesus really was raised from the dead, then the only possible, intellectually honest conclusion one can reach is that he really is who he claimed to be. If Jesus actually got up from the grave in the way the Bible says he did, then he really is the Son of God, the King of kings and Lord of lords, the Way, the Truth, the Life, and the Wisdom of God, just like he said. And if *that's* true, then it makes sense (doesn't it?) that he probably knows what he's talking about, and therefore, we ought to listen to him.

Now, one thing that is beyond any reasonable doubt is that Jesus believed the Bible. When it comes to the Old Testament, the point is very straightforward; over and over in his teaching, Jesus authenticated and endorsed it as the Word of God. And as for the New Testament, even though it was written years after his days on earth, it too rests ultimately on Jesus's own authority, and the early Christians knew it. In fact, the two main criteria they used to recognize authoritative books were (1) that those documents had to be authorized by one of Jesus's apostles and (2) that they had to agree in every particular with Jesus's own teaching. We'll talk more about all that later, but the point is pretty clear. Once you decide that Jesus really did rise from the dead, the truth and authority of the Bible follow quickly, naturally, and powerfully.

Now that's a quick and impressive case, I know, but here's the question: How exactly do you get it started? In other words, how do you get to the point of believing that Jesus really did rise from the dead in the first place? I mean, you can't just say you believe in the resurrection because the Bible says it happened, and you believe what the Bible says because Jesus rose from the dead, and you believe Jesus rose because you believe the Bible, and you believe the Bible because. . . . You probably get the point there, right? That whole thing would become just hopelessly and ridiculously circular. It reminds me of the little boy whose teacher asked him why the world doesn't just fall into space. "Because it's sitting on a turtle's back," the boy answered.

"And why doesn't the turtle fall?" the teacher asked.

"Because it's standing on another turtle's back," the boy insisted.

"And why doesn't that turtle fall?" the teacher pressed.

"Well," said the little boy thoughtfully, "obviously, it's turtles all the way down!"

Now before we go any farther, we should acknowledge that in one way or another, it's turtles all the way down for all of us, no matter what you take as your final authority for knowledge. So this issue affects everyone, not just Christians. If you ask a rationalist why he trusts reason, he'll say, "Because it's reasonable." If you ask a logician why she trusts logic, she'll say, "Because it's logical." If you ask a traditionalist why he trusts tradition, he'll say, "Because everyone has always trusted tradition." In all these cases, we're left crying out for more; why does one trust reason, logic, or tradition in the first place? Some may argue that reason is more reliable than spiritual explanations because you can see and touch the evidence in support of various claims. But even that argument rests on certain presumptions about what kind of evidence is or is not legitimate—that is, reasonable. You see? One way or another, you end up with turtles, all the way down, for everyone. In fact, I think that's probably one way God reminds us that we're finite—written deep in the logic of what it means to be human is an inescapable reminder that we can't figure it all out.

Even so, that doesn't mean we should give up all hope of knowing anything. Even if it's true in some philosophical, epistemological sense that we all ultimately have to stand on circular thinking, that doesn't mean we can't come to some confident conclusions about the nature of reality. Sure, some overzealous philosophers have at times thrown up their hands and said, "Well, that's it then! I guess we can't know anything!" But that kind of thinking tends to drop you into an episte-mological solitary-confinement cell (we can't know anything or anybody) that very few of us will find either inviting or necessary. So most of us simply start with a few presupposi-tions—for example, reason is reasonable, logic is logical, our senses are trustworthy, the world and we ourselves really exist and are not just "brains in a vat"—and then we proceed from those presuppositions to draw confident conclusions about ourselves, about history, about the world around us, about all sorts of things.

But hold on. The fact that we necessarily have to presup-pose *some things* doesn't mean we can presuppose *anything* we want. For example, you can't just presuppose that you're the president of the United States and work from there. Nor can you just presuppose that you're a god and that everything you happen to believe is therefore the case. Nor can you presuppose that the latest issue of the *National Enquirer* is the Word of God and that it therefore gives you an accurate picture of reality. These would be completely unwarranted presuppositions, and people would mock you for believing them—and perhaps lock you up as well! But here's the thing: More than a few people would say that's exactly what Christians have done with the Bible. We have, without any good reason whatsoever, simply presupposed that it is the Word of God, that everything it says is therefore true, and that Jesus therefore rose from the dead.

But what if the alleged foul is not quite that flagrant? What if there's a way to come to a good and confident conclusion that Jesus really did rise from the dead *without simply presupposing that the Bible is the Word of God*? If we could do this, then we'd be able to avoid the charge of unwarranted circularity. We'd be able to say that, *even before concluding that the Bible is the Word of God*, we came to a confident conclusion that Jesus did in fact rise from the dead, and then, on the basis of that confident conclusion, we followed him in accepting the Bible as the Word of God. This kind of belief would differ markedly from one that simply relied on a "leap of faith." Not only could it be defended against skeptics' objections; it could also challenge skeptics in their unbelief. It would be, as Peter wrote, a formidable "reason for the hope that is in [us]" (1 Pet. 3:15).

## Christianity as History

The question, of course, is whether there really is a way to do that. To cut right to the chase, I think there is, and I think it is by *doing history*. In other words, let's approach the documents that make up the New Testament not *first* as the Word of God but simply as historical documents, and then on that basis, let's see if we can arrive at a confident conclusion that Jesus rose from the dead. Even someone who's not a Christian should have no objection to this. After all, to approach the New Testament simply as a collection of historical documents involves no special pleading, no special status, no special truth claims. Let's let them speak for themselves in the "court of historical opinion," as it were.

Moreover, to approach the New Testament as historical shouldn't raise any particular objections among Christians. After all, it's not as if that would be to treat it as something *other than* what it is. The New Testament documents themselves claim to be historical; their authors intended them to be historical. Take Luke, for example. He began his Gospel by saying that he aimed to give his reader "an orderly account" of the life and teachings of Jesus (Luke 1:3). However you slice that, and whatever else you think Luke was doing, he was most certainly writing history. Of course, the method of writing history in the ancient world differed from our own method of doing so, but the basic idea was still the same—the authors were writing accounts of events that they believed really happened. So given that Luke and the other authors were doing that kind of work, surely there's nothing inappropriate about letting his books, and the others, stand and speak as what they were intended to be all along.

Even more, though, than the religions of the world, Christianity presents itself *as history*. It's not primarily just a list of ethical teachings or a body of philosophical musings or mystical "truths" or even a compendium of myths and fables. At its very heart, Christianity is a claim that something extraordinary has happened in the course of time—something concrete and real and *historical*.

## A Chain of Reliability

But even if that's so, another question arises at this point, and we'll spend most of this book trying to answer it: Are the New Testament documents—and especially, for our purposes, the four Gospels—truly *reliable* as historical witnesses? That is to say, can we trust them to give us good, dependable information about the events of Jesus's life, especially concerning his resurrection, such that we can end up saying, "Yes, I'm pretty confident that actually happened"? For my part, I think we *can* trust the New Testament documents, but getting to that conclusion will take some work, precisely because, as with any historical document, we can raise many questions at many different points about their reliability.

To understand what I mean by that, think of it like this. If you're reading, say, Matthew's Gospel about any particular event in the life of Jesus, you can count at least three different people who have put their hands on the biblical account you are reading and have therefore affected it in some way. First, and most obviously, the account originates with the author who wrote it down. Second, at least one person, and likely more, copied that original writing and thereby transmitted it, so to speak, through the centuries into our hands. Third, someone (or some committee) translated that copy from its original language into your native language so you can now read it. At each step in that process, questions arise that bear heavily on whether you can really trust the story you're reading to give a reliable account of what actually happened. So, moving backward in time from yourself to the event itself, you end up with a chain of five big questions:

1. Can we be confident that the *translation* of the Bible from its original language into our language accurately reflects the original, or is it saying things the original never did?

2. Can we be confident that copyists accurately *transmitted* the original writing to us, or did they (deliberately or not) add, subtract, or change things so much that what we have is no longer what was originally written?

3. Can we be confident that we're looking at the right set of books and that we haven't missed or lost a set of books out there that gives a different, but equally reliable and plausible, perspective on Jesus? That is, can we be confident that we're right to be looking at *these books* as opposed to those?

4. Can we be confident that the original authors were themselves *trustworthy*? That is, were they really intending to give us an accurate account of events, or did they have

some other aim—for example, to write fiction or even to deceive?

5. And finally, if we can be confident that the authors did, in fact, intend to give an accurate account of what happened, can we be confident that what they described really took place? In a word, can we be confident that what they wrote is actually *true*? Or are there better reasons to think that they were somehow mistaken?

Do you see? If we can respond to each of these questions— translation? transmission? these books? trustworthy? true?— with a firm "Check!" then we'll have a pretty solid chain of reliability from ourselves to the events in question. We'll be able to say, confidently, that

1. we have good translations of the biblical manuscripts;
2. those manuscripts are accurate copies of what was originally written;
3. the books we're looking at are indeed the right and best books to look at;
4. the authors of those documents really did intend to tell us accurately what happened; and
5. there's *no good reason to think they were mistaken* in what they saw and recorded.[1]

However you look at it, these affirmations would establish a pretty solid foundation for thinking that we really can accept the Bible as historically reliable. And if we can do that, then it

---

[1] This particular line of thought is an expansion of an approach I first learned from Mark Dever, pastor of Capitol Hill Baptist Church in Washington, DC. Other Christian authors have also used a similar approach.

follows that we can consider the Bible's account of the resurrection of Jesus and say, "Yes, I really do believe that happened. As much as I believe that any other event in history happened, I believe Jesus rose from the dead."

## A Few Important Thoughts

Now, let me say three more things before we start trying to build that kind of historical case. First, keep in mind that we're not searching for what we might call *mathematical certainty*. That kind of logical, lock-it-down certainty is possible in mathematics and sometimes in science, but it's *never* possible when you're dealing with history. With any historical event, someone somewhere will always be able to concoct an alternative to the accepted account that has at least a bare chance of being the case. "Maybe Caesar didn't in fact cross the Rubicon River," someone might say. "Maybe one of his generals *dressed* as Caesar and managed to fool everyone. Yes, yes, I know there's no good reason to think that, but it's still *barely* possible, and therefore you can't be confident that Caesar ever crossed the Rubicon." Okay, but for crying out loud, come on! If objections like that were enough to keep us from drawing firm conclusions about history, we'd never be confident in *any* knowledge about the past.

Thankfully, though, we're not looking here for mathematical certainty but rather for *historical confidence*. We want to be able to say not so much, "It is a mathematical, logical certainty that Caesar crossed the Rubicon," but rather, "Some people actually did report that Caesar crossed the Rubicon. We think they were intending to report what actually happened (rather than to deceive or mythologize), and there's no good reason to think they were mistaken in their report. Therefore, we can be historically confident that Caesar really did cross the Rubicon." That's the kind of "certainty" we look for in history, and to demand anything more is to demand something from historical study that it can never deliver.

Second, keep in mind that *historical confidence* provides sufficient grounds for *action*. Occasionally I've run into people who assert that they're not going to act on anything without firsthand experience of it. If they didn't see it or experience it, they say, then there's just too much doubt to act on it in any way. Now, at first glance, that position seems to have a sheen of intellectual respectability; it seems careful and thoughtful. But look at it a moment longer, and you realize that nobody actually lives like that, not *really*. The fact is, we all put confidence in—and *act on*—things of which we ourselves have no direct knowledge or experience all the time.

Think about it. I wasn't present when the Constitution of the United States was ratified, but as an American, I live with the confidence that it in fact *was*, and I also act on that confidence. I don't decline to vote because I'm not *mathematically certain* that we really live under a ratified US Constitution. Here's another example, even closer to home: When you get right down to it, I have no direct knowledge that my parents really are my parents; I don't personally remember my birth, we've never had a DNA test done, and it's always *possible* some mistake was made and my birth certificate was forged!

Well, sure, that's barely possible, but on the other hand, all the evidence I have points to the fact that my parents really are my parents, and so I live *and act* all the time with confidence that they are.

That's the kind of confidence history can provide, and it's the kind of confidence I hope we can reach as we think together throughout the pages of this book—a historical confidence that would allow us, even compel us, to say, "Yes, I think the resurrection of Jesus happened. I have no better explanation for the facts. And now I'm going to act on that confidence."

Third, please keep in mind that this is not and wasn't intended to be an academic book. It doesn't consider every possible variation on every argument, and it doesn't give every possible example or counterexample. For that reason, I hope you won't compare it to the many excellent books that Christians have written on all these topics over the years. If you set this book beside those, you'll find that it is not as thorough as those—or as thick. It aims simply to present a flyover of the arguments and considerations that have convinced me—and many others over the years—of the Bible's truth.

One more thing. In keeping the argument to that flyover level, you'll notice that I've focused particularly in this book on the New Testament—and within the New Testament, particularly on the four Gospels. That means I'm not going to treat every nuance of text, transmission, and canon that arises in discussions regarding the Old Testament or even regarding every book of the New Testament. But, you ask, isn't this book about the *whole* Bible? It is. Yet keep in mind that exploring the evidence for the New Testament, especially the Gospels, with the five tests above will give us a good sense of the issues and historical evidence involved in discussions of all the other books, too. And even more important, remember that what we're aiming for, finally, is historical confidence that Jesus rose from the dead. If we can arrive at that, then we wind up with a very good reason for trusting in the reliability of the Old Testament as well. So how do we arrive at historical confidence that Jesus was resurrected? By determining if the Gospels, in particular, are reliable historical witnesses. That's our aim.

So again, while other books helpfully discuss all the minute details of all the issues involved with the Bible's reliability at every point, this book presents an overview of the case that has convinced me and countless others of the Bible's truth—a case that finds its capstone in the resurrection of Jesus. If this case is helpful and, to some degree, convincing to you, I'm glad for that. If not, I'd encourage you to continue reading those other bigger, better books (see appendix).

## A First Step

If you're reading this book and you're not a Christian, first of all, thank you for picking it up and reading even this far. If nothing else, I hope you'll find some things in here that will challenge you to think about Christians, Christianity, the Bible, and ultimately Jesus in ways that are perhaps different than you have ever thought about them before. I hope you walk away recognizing that we Christians don't believe what we believe without reason. Sure, you may not buy the case I'm making here, but I hope you'll at least be able to say that maybe there's more to the Christian faith than you realized. On the other hand, you may even be able to say more than that. Maybe you'll come to the conclusion that you really *can* trust the Bible. If so, then you'll be in for a truly great experience, because you'll be able to turn confidently to thinking about what the Bible is really all about—Jesus the Christ and who he claimed to be.

On the other hand, if you're already a Christian, I hope this book will help you better understand *why* you trust the Bible and then enable you to talk about it and defend it against objections from people who do not trust it. The fact is, in the end, despite what the world often accuses us of, Christianity does not require people to make an irrational "leap of faith" that leaves them believing ridiculous things without evidence. On the contrary, our *actual* "leap of faith" consists in relying on Jesus to save us from our sins, precisely because he is eminently and solidly reliable.

And how do we know that?

Well, because the Bible tells us so.

Doesn't it?

# 2

# Lost in Translation?

Some years ago, I had the privilege of visiting Shanghai, China. Before my trip, some friends who lived there warned me not to assume that the English written underneath Chinese characters on many signs in the city would tell me anything about what the sign actually said. Over the years, Chinese translators had become notorious for mistranslating signs into English, with often misleading and sometimes even hilarious results.

I looked up some examples on the Internet before I left, and some of the mistranslations people have found are just funny. Take this sign hanging on the door of a restaurant: *Bar is presently open because it is not closed*. Or the menu that offers *Delicious Spicy Grandma* for your lunch entrée. Or the sign on a public lawn that just tugs at every heartstring you have: *Lovable but pitiful grass is under your foot*. Honestly, who knows what the original idea was behind any of those messages!

Having seen all that, I was, of course, looking forward to finding some amusing mistranslations myself. Sadly, I arrived in Shanghai just after the Summer Olympics had ended, and it turns out that the Chinese had launched a massive project to correct mistranslations throughout the country before the

Games started. So not even *once* did I get to sample any delicious spicy grandma for lunch or look into the sad face of some lovable but pitiful grass before I stepped on it!

But now, think about it for a moment. Why did China make sure to correct its foreign-language translations? It's simple—as the world turned its attention to their nation for the Olympics, they wanted to communicate accurately. They wanted to say what they meant, and they wanted to mean what they said. That's finally what is at stake in a translation, whether translating a sign, a menu, or the Bible. Can we be confident that what we're reading in our own language accurately reflects what the author meant to say in his?[1]

## Is Translation Even Possible?

The task of determining if the Bible really is historically reliable would be easier if we were native speakers of ancient Hebrew, ancient Aramaic, and ancient Greek. Most of us, however, are not. And that means we must not only ask whether the authors of the Bible were trustworthy and whether the copyists transmitted their writings accurately but also whether the Bibles we have in English are accurate translations of those copies.

Probably the first question we need to confront is whether the process of translation is even possible. Can we really take a language that looks like this,

---

[1] For this chapter, I have relied especially on Craig L. Blomberg, *Can We Still Believe the Bible?: An Evangelical Engagement with Contemporary Questions* (Grand Rapids, MI: Brazos, 2014); Paul D. Wegner, *The Journey from Texts to Translations: The Origin and Development of the Bible* (Grand Rapids, MI: Baker Academic, 1999).

Μὴ θησαυρίζετε ὑμῖν θησαυροὺς ἐπὶ τῆς γῆς, ὅπου σὴς καὶ βρῶσις ἀφανίζει, καὶ ὅπου κλέπται διορύσσουσιν καὶ κλέπτουσιν· θησαυρίζετε δὲ ὑμιν θησαυροὺς ἐν οὐρανῷ, ὅπου οὔτε σὴς οὔτε βρῶσις ἀφανίζει, καὶ ὅπου κλέπται οὐ διορύσσουσιν οὐδὲ κλέπτουσιν· ὅπου γάρ ἐστιν ὁ θησαυρός σου, ἐκεῖ ἔσται καὶ ἡ καρδία σου,

and have any confidence that this,

> Do not lay up for yourselves treasures on earth, where moth and rust destroy and where thieves break in and steal, but lay up for yourselves treasures in heaven, where neither moth nor rust destroys and where thieves do not break in and steal. For where your treasure is, there your heart will be also (Matt. 6:19–21),

means the same thing?

Well, the answer is, "Yes, but not without a lot of work." Any translation project requires years of effort first in understanding the meaning and structure of both languages and then in finding words and structures in the target language that accurately capture the meaning of the original. To put it less technically, translation is a matter of understanding the meaning of a word or sentence and then laboring to say the same thing in *different* words that will be understandable to a different person.

Now all that may sound hopelessly difficult, but if you think about it, even within our English language, we do this kind of thing all the time. For example, I have two sons who are nearing their teenage years, and I also have a father who would very much like to be able to communicate with his grandsons. Sometimes, though, believe it or not, that's significantly more difficult than you might imagine! It's not as if the three of them speak different languages either; they're all native English speakers. But even so, as the guy in the middle, I often find myself having to translate between them.

For example, when my son says something like, "Yo, it's chill, bro," my dad will look at me as if the boy has broken out in some ancient Egyptian or something. That's because, with the exception of the word *it's*, my father has absolutely no idea what any of the other words in that sentence mean. At that point, it's my job to start doing the work of *translation*—of thinking about the meaning of each word my son said and trying to come up with some *other* word or words that my dad will understand.

Now usually, I just translate the sentence all at once. "What he means, Dad, is that everything is okay. He's happy." But if I wanted to be really careful about it, I would need to explain each word in turn, like this:

- *Yo* is a customary but informal greeting in Kidspeak. Its Boomerspeak equivalent would be something like *hi* or *hey*.
- *Chill* in Kidspeak does not mean "cold." It communicates that a situation or a person is copacetic, happy, okay. It's actually a modern derivative of the common Boomerspeak word *cool*, as in "It's cool; I'm cool; everything is cool."
- *Bro* is a term of friendship and endearment, a shortened form of the word *brother*. But that doesn't mean a person has to be a blood relative to be your *bro*. It might best be

translated into Boomerspeak as *friend*, or more colloquially, *man*.

So, putting it all together, we can translate the Kidspeak sentence "Yo, it's chill, bro" into Boomerspeak as "Hey, it's all okay, man." And hearing that, my dad's eyes light up with understanding, he gives my son a smile and a thumbs-up, and they share a moment of genuine and accurate—though translated—communication. "That's gnarly!" my dad says. And then we're off to the translation races again!

I know, I know, that's a ridiculously simplistic picture of what the hard work of translation really requires, and those who do that work—whether we're talking about the Bible or any other great literature or even the translation necessary to make our global society work every day—they are heroes. The point I'm trying to make, even with this slightly outlandish example, is not that translation is easy or simple but that it's *possible*. It really is possible for genuine, accurate, correct communication to occur through translation.

This means no one can make a "case closed" objection to the historical reliability of the Bible simply because we're reading English translations of Greek and Hebrew documents. Scholars have been studying Greek, Hebrew, Aramaic, and English literally for centuries, and they are able to translate accurately and precisely between those four languages.

## Why So Many Bible Versions?

If that's true, then why are there so many different translations of the Bible? Go into any Christian bookstore, and you can find an entire shelf—sometimes an entire section!—of different Bible translations. There's the King James Version (KJV), the New King James Version (NKJV), and the Revised Standard Version (RSV). There's the Holman Christian Standard Bible (HCSB) and the English Standard Version (ESV) and the New Living Translation (NLT) and the New International Version (NIV). And then, to top it all off, many of these have other editions, like the military edition, the sports edition, the men's and women's and teenagers' and students' and businessperson's editions. Why?

Is it because the people who worked on the ESV thought the people who worked on the NIV got the Bible largely wrong? Or because the KJV committees translated the Bible so badly that the RSV translators had to correct it all? For that matter, does the book of John change when it addresses men, women, athletes, or soldiers?

In short, the answer to all these questions is "no." When it comes to the different editions of the Bible aimed at students or men or women or soldiers, all those are simply marketing packages in which the actual text of the Bible remains the same. They differ only in the additional items that accompany the text—the introductory content, the study notes, the devotional articles, and other material. There's no reason at all to think the presence of both a men's study Bible and a women's study Bible in your local bookstore introduces any confusion at all into the meaning of the biblical text.

But what about the various translations themselves? Don't they render the Bible so differently from each other that we really can't be sure at all about the original meaning? That's a good question, but in reality, even when different translations use different words to render the same Greek or Hebrew phrase, that does not necessarily—or even very often at all—leave us with any doubt about what the original was saying.

Think again about our example of the Kidspeak sentence, "Yo, it's chill, bro." I could have translated that sentence to my dad in a number of ways:

- "Hey, it's all good, man."
- "Listen, everything is okay, my friend."
- "You know what? The situation is copacetic, loved one."

The specific words differ in all these translations. But even so, is there really any doubt about what "Yo, it's chill, bro" is communicating? Whichever of these *translations* you use, what the sentence *means* is that my son wants someone with whom he is in a friendly relationship to be aware that he does not think his current situation is problematic; he's satisfied with it.

You can do the same sort of thing with verses in the Bible. Let's take one at random and look at how several translations render it. I just asked my wife to name one of the four Gospels. "Mark," she said.

"Now pick a number between one and fifteen."

"Ten!"

"And another number between one and fifty-two."

"Fifty!"

So let's look at Mark 10:50 and see how several English Bibles translate that verse. Here it is in the original Greek:

ὁ δὲ ἀποβαλὼν τὸ ἱμάτιον αὐτοῦ ἀναπηδήσας ἦλθεν πρὸς τὸν Ἰησοῦν.

The English Standard Version translates it like this:

And throwing off his cloak, he sprang up and came to Jesus.

Here's the New American Standard Bible:

Throwing aside his cloak, he jumped up and came to Jesus.

The New International Version:

Throwing his cloak aside, he jumped to his feet and came to Jesus.

The New Revised Standard Version:

So throwing off his cloak, he sprang up and came to Jesus.

And the King James Version:

And he, casting away his garment, rose, and came to Jesus.

Crazy, isn't it? How on earth are we ever going to get our heads around what Mark 10:50 is really saying? I mean, sure, everyone seems to agree that this man came to Jesus, but did he *throw* his cloak or *cast* it? Was it even a *cloak* at all, or was it a *garment*? And for crying out loud, how are we ever supposed to determine whether he *sprang, jumped,* or *rose* before he came to Jesus?

Alright, obviously I'm being facetious here. For all the differences between these five translations, it's really clear what's going on. The man quickly takes off his outer piece of clothing, gets up, and makes his way to Jesus. My point here is simply to say that different translations do not prevent us from knowing what the original actually meant. In fact, reading two or three translations side-by-side can many times actually help fill out the picture of what's happening.

Still, though, we need to go farther, because obviously not every verse in the Bible is quite as straightforward as Mark 10:50. Certain words and phrases are indeed difficult to translate, and in those cases, different translators will often disagree about how to render those words or phrases. But even in those instances, we should keep at least a handful of things firmly in mind:

1. Scholars significantly disagree about how to translate only an exceedingly small percentage of words or phrases in the Bible. These cases also represent an exceedingly small portion of any given book (or even any chapter) in the Bible.

2. When there is such disagreement or uncertainty, the best translations of the Bible will acknowledge that in a footnote, making the reader aware of other possible translations or even noting (as the ESV puts it) that "the meaning of the Hebrew [or Greek] is uncertain."[2] The point is, no

---

[2] See, for example, the ESV note on Isa. 10:27.

one is trying to "slip anything through" without telling us, nor—at this point in the history of English translations—would they be able to do so even if they wanted to.

3. The sheer number of scholarly translations actually helps us identify—and avoid!—deliberately misleading translations. For example, when the New World Translation (NWT) of the Jehovah's Witnesses translates John 1:1 as "and the Word was a god," it helps to be aware that every other major translation renders that verse "and the Word was God." Clearly, the NWT has done something here that the other translations reject, and if you studied Greek long enough to understand its use of articles (*a*, *an*, and *the*), you would come to the same conclusion the other translators obviously did—that the NWT has tailored its "translation" of that verse to protect a particular, idiosyncratic theological doctrine.

4. Once we identify and reject deliberate mistranslations like that, we can confidently say that not one major doctrine of orthodox Christianity rests on a disputed or uncertain translation of the Bible's original languages. We know what the Bible says, and we know what it means.[3]

But one more question arises. Why are there different translations of the Bible in the first place? If the significantly disputed portions of the text are so rare and if they don't affect any major doctrines, then why have people gone to so much expense and trouble to make all those translations? That's an

---

[3] For a more detailed treatment of all these points, see Blomberg, *Can We Still Believe the Bible?*, 83–118; Wegner, *Journey*, 399–404.

excellent question, and the answer comes down to recognizing all the different ways people use the Bible in their lives.

Think about it. People read the Bible devotionally, they preach from it, they use it in Bible studies, they do scholarly work on it, they study it, they have conversations about doctrines from it, they defend their understanding of the faith with it. And the fact is, for most of these activities, a strict word-for-word translation of the original Greek or Hebrew would not be very useful. In fact, it would be incredibly frustrating. Just take Mark 10:50 again. If we translated it strictly word-for-word from the Greek, it would come out sounding something like this:

> The but he throwing off the cloak his he jumped up he came to the Jesus.

Sure, you can puzzle it out, and maybe that kind of strict word-for-word translation would be useful if you're doing very careful scholarly work on that verse. But who wants to endure that when you just want to read the Bible over a cup of coffee in the morning?

That's the main reason we have different translations—for different uses of the Bible. Sometimes a stricter, more word-for-word translation of the original language is exactly what you need. But at other times, you want something a bit more readable, a bit more readily understandable, and so some translations offer a more phrase-for-phrase (or even thought-for-thought) approach, smoothing out word order, preferring English syntax over Greek or Hebrew syntax, and generally just rendering the thoughts of the original in a form that an English-speaking reader will better understand. To put it slightly more technically, every translation of the Bible has to aim, to one degree or another, at both *accuracy* and *readability*. Some translation committees take it as their mission to heavily privilege accuracy and (as we saw with Mark 10:50) necessarily sacrifice readability to a certain degree. Other translation committees set out to produce a version that is eminently readable, but that decision necessarily means the translators will have to rearrange some of the original language's word order so that the sentences will sound "right" to an English-language ear.

I hope you can see the point in all this. Nothing in either the theory or the reality-on-the-ground of Bible translations introduces the slightest bit of doubt about whether we can really know what the Bible in its original languages says. In fact, we *do* know what it says, and the places where some scholars disagree are few and far between and ultimately of minor significance. The Bible can be *and has been* translated correctly, over and over and over again.

Of course, in determining *historical reliability*, that only gets us so far. We next have to ask the question, Are we translating what the authors originally wrote?

In other words, did the people who copied the originals copy them correctly?

# 3

# Copies of Copies of Copies of Copies?

When I was in high school and college, I took a few foreign language courses. My favorite by far was Spanish, and though this won't sound impressive to you real scholars out there, by the end of it all I had spent *four whole academic years* studying that language. Fifteen years or so removed from those classes now, I'm not very good at Spanish anymore—reading it, speaking it, hearing it, anything. In the days when I was really working hard on it, though, I got pretty good at doing Spanish translations, both *from* and *to* English. Part of that was because my Spanish professor gave us translation homework *every single night*. Do you remember how most college classes were scheduled to meet every other day—either Monday-Wednesday-Friday or Tuesday-Thursday? Not Spanish. It was every day, Monday through Friday, which meant that every night I had a particular passage of either English or Spanish text that I had to translate into the other language and be ready to discuss in class the next day.

I was good at it too. By my senior year in college I could bang out a translation of several hundred words in just a couple of hours and be ready at a moment's notice to explain the syntax of each and every sentence. Once or twice, though, I learned a rough, painful lesson when I arrived at class: no matter how good my translations were, it didn't matter if I had looked at the wrong page and translated the wrong passage!

Sometimes people will make a similar charge about the Bible—that even if we *are* able to say confidently that we're translating *accurately*, there's no way we can be confident that we're translating *the right thing*, so it's all useless anyway. The charge is not so much that we have the *wrong* documents. It's that because we don't have the original documents written by the authors' own hands, the copies we do have must be hopelessly corrupt, and therefore we can't possibly know what the authors originally wrote. And if that's true, the argument goes, then it's meaningless to carry on the discussion any further.

One American magazine made this very point sharply:

No television preacher has ever read the Bible. Neither has any evangelical politician. Neither has the pope. Neither have I. And neither have you. At best, we've all read a bad translation—a translation of translations of translations of hand-copied copies of copies of copies of copies, and on and on, hundreds of times.[1]

Now, we've already dealt with the "bad translation" charge in this book; it's not true, and if that's not clear to you, perhaps

---

[1] Kurt Eichenwald, "The Bible: So Misunderstood It's a Sin," *Newsweek*, December 23, 2014, http://www.newsweek.com/2015/01/02/thats-not-what-bible-says-294018.html.

you should go back and read chapter 2 again. Moreover, it's also not true that we're dealing with "a translation of translations of translations," as if the original Greek first went into Chinese, which went into German, which went into Polish, and finally we got around to putting it into English. No, we're able to translate directly from the original Greek and Hebrew into English and other languages, so at worst we're dealing with a *translation*, full stop. But what should we say about that last idea, the charge that all we have available to us are "hand-copied copies of copies of copies of copies?"

Copypock. Er, I mean, poppycock. That's what we should say.

## We Don't Have the Originals—So What Now?

Let's think about the question of *transmission*—that is, can we be confident that the original text of the Bible was transmitted accurately to us through the centuries? As we consider this question, right off the bat we should acknowledge the gigantic glittering elephant standing in the room: we don't have the originals.[2]

Whatever pieces of paper Luke, John, and Paul used to write the Gospel of Luke, the Gospel of John, and the epistle to the Romans have been lost to history. (Technically, they would have most likely used papyrus or vellum, and later scribes would have employed parchment, but *paper* suffices as shorthand in this book.) And it's highly unlikely that we will ever

[2] For this chapter, I have relied especially on Craig L. Blomberg, *Can We Still Believe the Bible? An Evangelical Engagement with Contemporary Questions* (Grand Rapids, MI: Brazos, 2014); Paul D. Wegner, *The Journey from Texts to Translations: The Origin and Development of the Bible* (Grand Rapids, MI: Baker Academic, 1999).

find a biblical manuscript about which we can say, "We are 100 percent certain that this is the original piece of paper on which the author wrote." But before we throw our hands up and drop into despair, let's think about that point for a minute. How important is it, really, that we have *the original piece of paper*? I mean, it would definitely be neat. When I visited London a few years ago, I attended the exhibition *Treasures of the British Library*, which displayed some of the most valuable cultural and historical artifacts in the world, the most treasured and sacred relics that the curators could dig out of the hallowed archives of the British Library. It was an amazing collection. Right there displayed before me were Magna Carta; Gutenberg's Bible of 1455; Handel's *Messiah* written in his own hand; Codex Sinaiticus, the earliest known complete copy of the New Testament; Leonardo da Vinci's notebook; and (silence please) the original lyrics to the Beatles song "Help!" as John Lennon scratched them onto a piece of scrap paper.

Ladies and gentlemen, I'm very pleased to announce that we *know*, beyond a shadow of doubt, the original lyrics to "Help!" as the Beatles wrote them. We can *see* them on the napkin. And in its way, I admit that's very cool. I'm not sure it reaches the *Treasures of the British Library* level of cool, but it's cool nonetheless.

But here's the thing. Is possessing *the original piece of paper* the only way we can have any confidence that what we *do* have is in fact what the authors themselves wrote? I mean, are we forever doomed to say that we don't really have any idea what Homer or Plato wrote because we don't have the pieces of paper on which they wrote *The Odyssey* or *The Republic?* Is "Help!" the only Beatles song we'll ever *really* know the lyrics to? Certainly not! And to say so would be ridiculously pedantic. So what about the documents of the Bible? Are we really left simply to give up and admit that we only possess a bunch of useless copies of copies of copies of copies and that we'll never have any confidence that the remaining copies accurately reflect what the authors actually wrote?

Well, no, we're not left to that despairing conclusion. In fact, even though we don't have the Bible's *original pieces of paper*, we can in fact be highly confident that we know what those original pieces of paper said. Now how can that be?

The key to answering that question lies in the fact that even though we don't have the originals, we do have thousands of *other* pieces of paper (again, technically, papyrus, vellum, and parchment) that contain original-language text from each book of the Bible—about 5,400 distinct pieces when it comes to the New Testament. We're not even talking here about pieces of paper from modern printing presses; we're talking about *ancient* manuscripts from before the invention of the printing press, some of which go back to the third century or even (perhaps?) earlier. Some of those manuscripts contain whole copies of biblical books; others have been partially destroyed so that only portions of books remain. Still others are literally mere fragments of what were once much larger manuscripts. Again, none of these documents are the originals of the Bible; they're all copies of something older. But we've found them scattered all over what used to be the Roman Empire, hidden in caves, buried in ancient ruins, or even—believe it or not—deposited in the ancient trash heaps of an abandoned Egyptian city! Moreover, once experts dated these fragments of text, we discovered that they hail from the first three or four centuries of Christian history.[3]

Now what makes all these manuscripts and fragments interesting—or problematic, depending on how you look at it—is that at certain places they *differ* from each other, even when they're supposed to be copies of the same exact portion of the Bible. So, for example, one manuscript of Matthew's Gospel quotes Pontius Pilate as saying, "I am innocent of this man's blood" (Matt. 27:24), while a fragment of the same book from another place or from a later century quotes Pilate as saying, "I am innocent of this righteous blood," while still another quotes him as saying, "I am innocent of this righteous man's blood."[4] So what gives? Obviously, at least once and perhaps more than once, someone inaccurately copied the original words that Matthew wrote.

Some people look at all this—the 5,400 manuscripts or fragments with all their variations—and say, "No way. There's *no way* we can know what the originals said. The surviving copies are too far removed and too corrupted for us to have any confidence at all that we know what the authors originally wrote." That conclusion, though, just goes way too far. Here's why. For one thing, the problems that skeptics often cite as arising from all this—that the manuscripts we have are too far

---

[3] For detailed information on extant New Testament manuscripts, see, for example, Wegner, *Journey*, 235–42.
[4] See the ESV textual note on Matt. 27:24.

removed in time from the originals and that they're absolutely riddled with variations—are not nearly so bad as some people make them out to be. And for another thing, it turns out that it's *precisely* the existence of those thousands of copies, from all over the empire and with all their variations, that allows us to reconstruct with a *huge degree of confidence* what the originals said.

Let me try to explain all that, one step at a time.

## Mind the Gap!

First of all, the charge is often made that the documents we have are so hopelessly removed in time from the originals that we might as well give up trying to figure out what the originals said. After all, the New Testament originals were all written in the mid-to-late first century, and the earliest copies we have of various portions are from about AD 125, 150, and 200. That means that for at least some portions of the New Testament, the gap between the originals and our earliest-surviving copies may be only forty-five to seventy-five years. Now that sounds fairly problematic to most of us because, for some reason, we imagine that seventy-five years is a lot of time—enough time in fact for copies of copies of copies to be made and subsequently lost so that we have no idea what the originals actually looked like. But that's not a fair assumption at all, especially when you realize that books in general were far more valuable to ancient people than they are to us today and that they, therefore, probably kept better care of them than we do. Even now, when we're able to print books every year by the millions, you can walk into just about any used bookstore and find books that are one or two or even three hundred years old. People make their books last! And that was even more the case in ancient times, when literally *weeks* of labor would go into copying a book. Scholars have learned from looking in old libraries that people regularly used books for 100–150 years before making a new copy and discarding the old.

We see one fascinating example of this practice in what we call the Codex Vaticanus, a copy of the New Testament that was originally made in the fourth century but that scribes re-inked in the tenth century so it could continue to be used. Do you see what that means? Codex Vaticanus was still in use *six hundred years* after it was originally made! Here's the point: when books were regularly kept in use for literally hundreds of years, a gap of forty-five to seventy-five years between the original New Testament documents and our earliest extant (*extant* means *surviving* or *existent*) copies is just not that long. In fact, it's more than a little likely that the originals, penned by the authors themselves, would have been preserved and used to make countless new copies over decades or even centuries before they were lost. Therefore the claim that all we have are "copies of copies of copies of copies" of the originals is far overwrought.

Also, when you consider the gap that exists between the originals and the earliest extant copies of other ancient works, you can see very quickly just how small the "gap" for the New Testament really is. For example, for Plato's *Tetralogies*, we currently have only about two hundred manuscripts, the earliest of which is some thirteen hundred years removed from the original! For Julius Caesar's *Gallic Wars*, we have a total of nine or ten readable copies (depending on your sense of what's "readable"), the earliest of which dates nine hundred years later than the original. For Tacitus's *Histories* and *Annals*, written in the first century, two manuscripts survive, one dating from the ninth century and the other from the eleventh—eight hundred and one thousand years, respectively, later than the extant copies. You can easily see the point here: No one screams, "Mind the gap!" when it comes to other ancient literature. Only the New Testament receives that kind of treatment.

## Five Hundred Thousand Differences?

On to the second charge, that the manuscripts we do have are so riddled with differences, or variants, that it's hopeless to think we can ever have any confidence about what the originals said. Some scholars have estimated that the New Testament manuscripts available to us contain up to 500,000 variants. (The reason we have to say "up to" is that nobody has actually sat down to count, and there are disagreements, too, on *how* to count—what counts as a difference, for instance, or whether you should count each word in a phrase or the entire phrase as one variant. The point is that any proposed number of "variants" is at best an educated guess—some scholars say there are 200,000; others, 500,000.) How do these differences affect how much confidence we can place in the New Testament documents?

Let's assume for the sake of argument that the 500,000 number is accurate; in fact, that's a pretty good estimate. At first glance, that sounds like a bewilderingly large number, as if the documents are just riddled with differences. After all, the New Testament has only about 138,000 words in its entirety! But after closer examination, I think you'll see that the documents are *not* in fact hopelessly riddled with variants.

First, not all 500,000 of those variants have an equal chance of being correct. In fact, a huge portion of them are either total nonsense (meaning that scholars can quickly agree that a copyist just made a mistake) or singular (meaning that a particular variant shows up in one and only one manuscript, likely an error by a single copyist). To put this in perspective, scholars have estimated that singular variants alone make up about 45 percent of those 500,000. Add the obviously nonsensical variants, and it turns out we're talking not about 500,000 but about 275,000 significant differences in our manuscripts.

Now admittedly, that still sounds like a big number, and some critics of the Bible will say something like, "There are only 138,000 words in the whole New Testament, so you have twice as many variants as you do actual words!" If you think about it, though, that's not a fair comparison. The copyists who introduced 500,000 variants didn't write just 138,000 words; they wrote *millions* of words over 5,400 extant manuscripts. Of course, we don't know exactly how many millions—again, no one has counted them all—but let's do a little math on one particular passage that someone *has* counted.

In the Greek language, John 18 has 791 words, and the manuscripts we have of that chapter include 3,058 variations. Is it fair, then, to say that there are 3.9 variations per word in John 18? Of course not! Those 3,058 variations are spread over 1,659 manuscripts of John 18. If we can assume that those 1,659 manuscripts have an average of 791 words each, then those 3,058 variations are spread over some 1,312,296 words that the copyists actually wrote! Even more, when you consider that 1,767 of those 3,058 are singular variations, and another 187 are obviously nonsensical, you wind up with 1,104 significant variants over 1,312,296 words—or just 1 for every 1,188 words![5]

The point is that statistics can be considered in many different ways, and so a headline screaming simply that there are "500,000 variants in the New Testament" shouldn't make us declare the whole thing to be hopeless. When you consider how many of those variants are obviously nonsense, how many are simple spelling mistakes, how many make no difference to the meaning, *and* how many manuscripts they're spread over, it's clear that you have to think more deeply than just the bare number itself. At the same time, our confidence that we know what the original documents of the New Testament said doesn't come from *counting* variants at all but from *comparing* them.

---

[5] For more details and for the numbers used in this section, see Peter Gurry, "The Number of Variants in the Greek New Testament: A Proposed Estimate," *New Testament Studies* 62, no. 1 (2016): 97–121. See also Blomberg, *Can We Still Believe the Bible?*, 13–28.

## Like Solving a Logic Puzzle

Believe it or not, at any given point in the New Testament where variants occur, it is precisely the existence of those variants that allows us to piece together what the original document most likely said.

Using variants to figure out what the original said is a lot like solving a logic puzzle. And the whole thing rests on the notion that when variants appear in the copies, we can usually identify not only *that* a scribe introduced a variation into his copy but also *why* he did so. Scribes introduced variants for all kinds of reasons. Sometimes it was purely accidental. For example, 1etters that looked similar miqht be switcheb out for each other; one word might be substituted for another won that sounded the same when read; words might skipped; words or letters might be be doubled; even whole sections might be skipped when the same word was used a few lines apart. (Go ahead, read that sentence again . . . there be Easter eggs hidden there!)

At other times, the changes introduced were very deliberate. So a scribe might decide that a word or name was misspelled and "correct" it; he might change something in one passage so that it would agree with another passage or even "fix" a word or two to clear up "problems" he perceived; or he might add something to the text in order to "clarify" what the reader should take from it.

Now here's where the fun starts, because once you can identify *why* a scribe made a certain change as he copied, you can get a very good idea of what the original said before he changed it. Here's a very simple example: Imagine that all you have is a fragment of a copy of a lost manuscript that reads, "Roses are read, violets are blue." It's not that hard to see what happened as the original was copied, is it? If we can give the original author the benefit of the doubt that he didn't write the nonsense phrase "Roses are read," then we can pretty confidently say that the scribe who made the copy simply misspelled the word *red* and that the original said, "Roses are red, violets are blue."

Here's a slightly more complicated example. Let's say you have two fragments, both copies of a long-lost original. One of those copies (we'll call it fragment A) reads:

> Now we are engaged in a great civil war. We have come to dedicate a portion of that field, as a final resting place for those who here gave their lives that that nation might live.

The other copy (fragment B) reads:

> Now we are engaged in a great civil war, testing whether that nation, or any nation so conceived and so dedicated, can long endure. We are met on a great battle-field of that war. We have come to dedicate a portion of that field, as a final resting place for those who here gave their lives so that the nation of which we speak might live.

Alright. Go ahead and take a minute or two to figure out the variations at issue here. There are two of them. Then read on.

Okay, did you see them? Most noticeably, fragment A is significantly shorter. It leaves out the entire segment "testing whether that nation, or any nation so conceived and so dedicated, can long endure. We are met on a great battle-field of that war." Also, the two fragments disagree about the last sentence. Did the original speak of those who gave their lives "so that that nation might live" or "so that the nation of which we speak might live"?

Let's start with the first variation, the omitted phrase about meeting on "a great battle-field" of the war. Is there any good reason to think that a copyist would *add* all those words to an original that didn't include them? Not really; at least I can't think of any. So if not, is there anything that might explain why he would *omit* them? Yes. See how the word *war* shows up twice in fragment B? In fact, those two occurrences kind of bracket the words that were omitted in fragment A. If the word *war* occurred twice in the original as well (especially if both times it appeared, say, at the end or beginning of a line), then that would provide a natural and easy place for the copyist's eye to "skip" accidentally from one occurrence to the other, and that would explain why he would have inadvertently omitted the words between them. Given that logic, we can pretty confidently say that the longer reading, in fragment B, more likely reflects the original.

What about the second variation? Is there any good reason why a copyist would amend an original that said "that the nation of which we speak might live" to "that that nation might live"? Probably not. After all, the phrase "that that nation" is just awkward. Therefore it's more likely that a copyist would "correct" the "that that" phrasing to something less grating on the ear. For that reason, we should probably conclude that the *harder* reading in fragment A reflects the original.

Given all this, we can come to solid conclusions that fragment B probably reflects the original on the first variation (because the copyist's eye skipped from "war" to "war") and that fragment A reflects the original on the second variation (because a copyist wouldn't "correct" the original to say "that that.") Therefore, we should reconstruct the original like this:

> Now we are engaged in a great civil war, **testing whether that nation, or any nation so conceived and so dedicated, can long endure. We are met on a great battle-field of that war.** We have come to dedicate a portion of that field, as a final resting place for those who here gave their lives *that that* nation might live.

Do you see? Just by reasoning through *why* copyists might make certain changes, we're able to arrive at a confident conclusion about what the original document actually said, *even though our final version is not entirely reflected in* either *of the fragments we actually have.* Neat, huh?

Well, that's exactly the kind of work scholars have done for centuries on the fragments and manuscripts of the New Testament available to us. Many of the puzzles they face, of course, are far more complicated than these simple examples, but you get the idea. By comparing the surviving ancient copies and thinking carefully about why copyists might have made certain changes or errors, scholars can reach highly confident conclusions about what the original documents actually said.

It's not a matter of guesswork or magic, much less of assumption or simply "making things up," but rather of careful deductive reasoning.

An actual example from the New Testament might help make the point. Existing manuscripts differ as to whether Matthew 5:22 originally read,

> But I say to you that everyone who is angry with his brother will be liable to judgment.

or

> But I say to you that everyone who is angry with his brother *without cause* will be liable to judgment.

The variation is clear, and so is the solution. What scribe would *delete* the words "without cause" when those words actually make this teaching of Jesus so much more palatable? Probably not many. Far more likely is that a scribe choked intellectually on the bare idea that someone who is angry with his brother would be liable to judgment and decided to "help Jesus out" by "clarifying" his teaching with the phrase "without cause." Because it's the harder reading, therefore, the first option most likely reflects the original. And for that reason, almost all the major translations leave out the phrase "without cause," simply putting it in a footnote at the bottom of the page.

## We Know What They Wrote

Before we conclude this issue, we should make another point or two. First, it's worth noting that the vast majority of the textual variants in the manuscript copies we have are just utterly uninteresting and undramatic. They have to do with plural versus singular pronouns, inverted word order, subjunctive versus indicative mood, aorist versus perfect tense, and on and on and on. Booooring! The vast majority don't actually include anything that affects how we ultimately understand the meaning of the Bible.

Second, Christian scholars have been exceedingly careful to document—in actual books that you can buy, if you're willing to shell out the money—the most significant variants *along with* an analysis of each one like the kind we've done here in this chapter. Of course you're free to disagree with any of their conclusions; Christians have fun arguing about this kind of thing all the time, believe it or not. But the point is that, again, there's no conspiracy to pull the wool over anyone's eyes. Where variants need to be reckoned with, Christians are wide open about them, precisely because we believe that those variants—and the reasons behind why they exist in the first place—can help us determine to a remarkably high degree of probability what the original documents of the New Testament actually said.

Finally, as with the issue of translation, it turns out that not a single doctrine of orthodox Christianity depends solely on a questioned portion of the biblical text. Either the questioned portions don't involve anything truly interesting, or if they do, the very same doctrines expressed in those locations are taught elsewhere in *unquestioned* portions of the Bible.

Do you see the point? The charge that we cannot know what the originals said is patently and utterly false. The gap between the originals and our earliest extant copies of them is—in the grand scheme of things—not that long at all. And far from *diminishing* our ability to identify what the originals said, the vast number of existing copies actually allows us to reason out deductively, to a very high degree of historical confidence, what John, Luke, Paul, and the other writers of the New Testament actually wrote.

## Where We've Come So Far

So here's where we've come so far in our investigation of whether the New Testament documents are historically reliable. First, we can indeed be confident that our translations of the documents are accurate and correct. Second, we can also be confident that we know what the authors of those documents originally wrote.

Translation? Check.

Transmission? Check.

But we're not done yet. Even if we can be confident that our translations are accurate and even if we can know to a high degree of certainty what the authors actually wrote, are we sure that we're looking at the right collection of documents?

In other words, why are we so convinced that we should be looking at *these* documents, and not *those*?

# 4

# Are These Really the Books You're Looking For?

I read *The Da Vinci Code*. I enjoyed reading *The Da Vinci Code*. As a page-turner of an action novel, it was a lot of fun. I stayed up late following the heroes as they traced clue after clue, puzzling out ancient riddles and traveling all over Europe. As of the writing of this book, Google tells me that *The Da Vinci Code* has sold over eighty million copies since its publication. Part of that success, I imagine, stems from Dan Brown's aptitude for storytelling, but that can't fully explain it. Nor can we point to the soaring literary quality of the book; that's not what sold it either. No, what sold *The Da Vinci Code* is what every author *dreams* will happen to one of his or her books—it ignited a worldwide controversy.

Most of the sensational story that Brown weaves was never taken seriously by most people. After all, *The Da Vinci Code* says right on its front page, "All the characters and events in this book are fictitious, and any resemblance to actual persons, living or dead, is purely coincidental." But the massive popularity of the book drove some of its claims deep into our collective understanding, even including those of us who are Christians. One of those claims is that the Bible as we know it is a purely artificial collection of books, perhaps even one tainted by conspiracy and power plays and evil scheming. Here's how one passage of *The Da Vinci Code* reveals the plot:

> "Who chose which gospels to include?" Sophie asked.
>
> "Aha!" Teabing burst in with enthusiasm. "The fundamental irony of Christianity! The Bible, as we know it today, was collated by the pagan Roman emperor Constantine the Great."[1]

That's a pretty ham-handed way of putting it, but the story Brown is peddling here has a long pedigree among scholars who are skeptical of the Bible. The picture that emerges is that for the first three centuries or so of the church's existence, a massive array of documents vied for attention and authority all over the Roman Empire. Each community of believers, so the story goes, had their own set of documents that they regarded as reflecting the true teaching of Jesus, and Christianity was a roiling, boiling, frothing cauldron of beautiful diversity and the glorious clash of ideas! Then, one dark day in the middle of the fourth century, a powerful cabal of sour-faced bishops gathered together in a small beach-resort town called Nicaea (typical, isn't it?), and with the backing of their rich patron, the pagan emperor Constantine, put a swift stop to it all. Publishing a list of the documents *they* liked best, these bishops forbade the

---

[1] Dan Brown, *The Da Vinci Code: A Novel* (New York: Doubleday, 2003), 231.

use of any others and began a program of systematically wiping out any dissent and destroying any documents that would dare provide a perspective on Jesus that differed from their own. Thus the "canon" of the New Testament was closed—like the door of a prison—and the world was plunged into darkness.

I may have added an embellishment or two there for drama's sake, but I think that's a pretty good description of the "movie" that plays in many people's heads when you raise the question of the biblical canon and what really belongs in it. At the very least, most Christians I know would have a hard time giving a confident answer to the question, "Are you sure you're looking at the right books?"

That's an important question too, because if our aim is to arrive at a confident conclusion that the Bible is historically reliable, we naturally have to be confident that we're looking at the right documents. If someone really did squelch, crush, destroy, burn, or otherwise suppress *other* books that tell a different *but equally reliable* story about Jesus, then our confidence that the Bible gives us a historically accurate story necessarily weakens considerably.

So that's the question we need to address in this chapter: Are these the right documents to be looking at in the first place? In other words, are there (or perhaps *were* there) other "Gospels" out there that we ought to be looking at as well—or even instead? How can we have any confidence that *these* are the right documents to be looking at and that others are not?[2]

---

[2] For this chapter, I have relied especially on Craig L. Blomberg, *Can We Still Believe the Bible? An Evangelical Engagement with Contemporary Questions* (Grand Rapids, MI: Brazos, 2014); F. F. Bruce, *The Canon of Scripture* (Downers Grove, IL: IVP Academic, 1988); C. E. Hill, *Who*

## What Is a Canon?

When we talk about the biblical *canon*, what we mean is the list of books that are accepted by Christians as, among other things, authoritative sources of information about Jesus. The word *canon* actually comes from the Greek language, where it refers to a *rule* or *standard*. You can see why Christians would come to use that word to refer to their collection of authoritative books; these are the documents that together and exclusively represent the *standard* by which the life and doctrine of Christians are to be measured, shaped, evaluated, and, if necessary, corrected. The question, of course, is how exactly that canon—that list of authoritative books—came about. Did that process give us confidence to rely on these books to give us accurate information about what really happened?

Because our initial aim is to arrive at historical confidence about the resurrection of Jesus, we don't need to spend much time now describing and defending the canon of the Old Testament.[3] We'll return to that question in chapter 7. For now, it suffices to say that by the time of Jesus, the Old Testament canon enjoyed near universal agreement, and both Jesus and his early followers accepted that canon without question.

For our purposes, the real issue is how the New Testament canon came to be. Much is at stake because these events bear strongly on how much historical confidence we can have in

*Chose the Gospels? Probing the Great Gospel Conspiracy* (Oxford: Oxford University Press, 2010); Paul D. Wegner, *The Journey from Texts to Translations: The Origin and Development of the Bible* (Grand Rapids, MI: Baker Academic, 1999).

[3] For a detailed treatment of the canon of the Old Testament and particularly the debate over the Apocrypha, see Wegner, *Journey*, 101–30; F. F. Bruce, "Old Testament," part 2 in *The Canon of Scripture*.

these documents. Here's why. If the New Testament canon resulted from a nasty conspiracy by powerful people who suppressed other books that had an equal claim to accuracy, then it would be very hard to conclude that the New Testament as it stands is historically reliable. Also, if they recognized these particular books on purely arbitrary grounds—that is, if they had no good reasons for it—then it would be similarly difficult to say that these books give us an accurate, reliable picture of Jesus. Finally, the same could be said if the process was essentially mystical. That is, if there are no *historically accessible reasons* for privileging these books and not others except, say, a personal "feeling" about their truthfulness, then we won't be able to have much historical confidence in them. To put it simply, if we're going to have historical confidence in what the New Testament documents tell us, then we have to ask, "Are our reasons for looking at these books, as opposed to others, sound?"

To cut to the chase, yes, they are sound. Getting to that conclusion, though, will take some work. We really need to do two things. First, we need to dispense with the idea that so many people adopted in the wake of *The Da Vinci Code*—that the New Testament canon was created by a conspiracy of powerful bishops who acted nastily and unfairly to suppress a bunch of equally noteworthy documents. And second, we need to ask if the early Christians had good reasons for privileging the documents they finally did. If there was no conspiracy to suppress other documents and if the early Christians had good reasons to privilege the documents they did, then we'll be able to say with good confidence that we are, in fact, looking at the right books.

## A Whole Sea of Gospels?

Let's start by considering whether there was a conspiracy to suppress other documents. Slice it however you want, that idea is nothing but arrant nonsense, and there are at least a couple of reasons for thinking so.

First of all, it's just not true that the early church was awash in a sea of books displaying a rainbowlike diversity of belief and that they responded (as some colorfully put it) by clearing a forest of perfectly good books in order to leave only their favorites standing. Early Christians simply didn't hold a vast diversity of beliefs. In fact, the *only* Christian writings that have been confidently dated to the first century are the very ones that finally made up the New Testament. Not only that, but the next oldest books—dated to the first half of the second century—were written by a group of teachers we've come to call the apostolic fathers, and all those guys were overwhelmingly in doctrinal agreement with the books that eventually made up the New Testament. Only in the latter part of the second century—a hundred years after most of the books that finally made up the New Testament were written—did documents start showing up that departed significantly from the teaching of these earliest books. And even then, those later works show an awareness of the earlier books, which marks them out as mere challengers to a strong, accepted tradition.

So what's the point here? The idea that there was a roiling, boiling sea of "Gospels" and other documents to choose from in the first two centuries of Christian history is simply untrue. There were the books of the New Testament, and then—a century later—there were the books that emerged trying to challenge them.

Second, the conspiracy theories all depend on this roiling, boiling sea persisting for several centuries before fourth-century bishops shut it down, but the church seems to have recognized the books of our New Testament as authoritative much earlier than any conspiracy theory's timeline allows. Usually, skeptics claim that no canon existed until some council or bishop codified it in the fourth century. But actually, the evidence shows that, although the church debated the authority of a handful of New Testament books into the fourth century, Christians widely recognized the vast majority of what we know as our New Testament as authoritative no later than the end of the second century. In fact, they widely recognized most of these books (including most of Paul's writings) as having such authority by the end of the *first* century.

When it comes to the four Gospels themselves—Matthew, Mark, Luke, and John—we have good reasons to think that the church had identified them as exclusively authoritative very early on, much earlier than the fourth century. One very interesting witness to this discussion is the bishop Irenaeus of Lyons, who wrote in about AD 180 that it was fitting for God to give the church four Gospels because there are four corners of the earth and four winds. Now, over the years, some people have had no end of fun mocking Irenaeus on this point; what sort of moron, they say, makes the claim, "There are four winds, so of course there must be four Gospels"? How does he expect that to convince anyone? But come on. Irenaeus isn't trying to make a *logical* argument here. He's not mainly trying to *convince* skeptics with this reasoning. No, what he's doing is making an *aesthetic* point about how beautiful and fitting and right it is that Christians have *four* Gospels, a point that would resonate primarily with people who *were already convinced* and needed only to be confirmed in that conviction. And therein lies the historical point. That Irenaeus would make that kind of argument—not so much trying to persuade skeptics as rejoicing with and affirming already-true believers—shows a widespread recognition, all the way back in AD 180, that there were indeed *four Gospels* and *only* four Gospels.

But the thread doesn't end there. Going back even further, the apologist Justin Martyr (writing in about AD 150) seems to have accepted four authoritative Gospels, as did a fellow named Papias writing as early as AD 110. And to top it off, there's even some intriguing evidence that Papias cited *the apostle John himself* as accepting the three other Gospels as well as writing one of his own.[4]

Here's the point. The commonly accepted picture of early Christianity as a frothy hotbed of diverse gospel writers and epistle writers, all vying equally for acceptance until a bunch of fourth-century bishops and their pagan emperor shut them down and wiped them out, is just sell-a-book nonsense. The

---

[4] For this argument, see Hill, *Who Chose the Gospels?*, 207–25.

historical reality is that the vast majority of the New Testament documents, especially the four Gospels, were identified and recognized as authoritative extremely early on, and writings claiming to "challenge" that general consensus only started showing up a century or so later. Now if that's true, then we've taken an important step toward establishing historical confidence in the New Testament canon: there simply was no conspiracy to privilege those books and suppress other "equally plausible but embarrassing" ones.

## They Didn't Choose—They Received

Even so, another question remains. Even if the New Testament documents weren't canonized under false or malevolent pretenses, we have to ask if the early Christians ultimately had plausible, historically valid reasons for choosing the documents they did for canonization.

But hold up. I just badly misspoke in the previous paragraph. The early Christians would actually *never* have talked about themselves "choosing" which books should be included in the canon. You might as well ask them, "Why did you choose the parents you did?" as "Why did you choose the books you did?"

The fact is, those early Christians simply didn't think of it like that at all. Over and over again when they wrote about which books were included in the canon and which were not, they used language such as "we *received*" and "these books were *handed down*." Their understanding of their role in the process was not that of a judging, pointing, *choosing* finger but rather that of an upturned, open, *receiving* hand.

Look, this isn't just a semantic point either, or even a spiritual one (yet). It's a historical one, and it bears heavily on our mental picture of how the process of canonization happened. The idea that the early church "chose" which books to canonize implies that they started with a blank slate and a group of undifferentiated books and then began a process of evaluating those books and deciding which ones they should privilege. But it never happened like that, not for a single one of the early Christians. In fact, every one of them—indeed, every generation—began not with a blank slate but rather with a group of authoritative books that they had *inherited* from the previous generation and which that generation in turn had inherited from the generation before them and so on and so on all the way back to the apostles themselves. True, occasionally someone would challenge that inherited set of books in one way or another, and the Christians would have to deal with that. But the fact remains that they simply didn't talk about *choosing* or *deciding* but only about *receiving what was handed down*. Theirs was a fundamentally humble posture. They received; they did not choose.

## They Had Good Reasons

Still, we can ask how those early Christians could remain *so* confident that the writings they recognized as authoritative were indeed the right ones. When challenges to the inherited tradition arose—some saying that this or that book *didn't* belong, others insisting that this or that book *did* belong—how did they answer? Did the early Christians have any solid criteria for saying, "Yes, we're actually very confident this received book belongs, and here's why," or, "No, we're quite sure that book does not belong, and here's why it fails"? In other words, did they just *blindly* receive what was handed down to them, or did they have good, plausible reasons for accepting those books?

The answer is that they did, in fact, have such reasons—such criteria—and four of them seem to have become their primary tests: apostolicity, antiquity, orthodoxy, and universality.

If we had time and space, we would simply canvass all the early sources in which Christians discussed *why* the church should or should not receive certain books as authoritative, and through that study we would see these four criteria (and others) emerge. We don't, however, have that time or space—this is a short book after all! Fortunately, one early document exhibits at least three of these four criteria being used in one place. That document, called the Muratorian Canon (or Muratorian Fragment), is a seventh- or eighth-century Latin translation of a document that was written originally in Greek probably in the late second century. You can see the full text of it in any good, comprehensive book on the canon (see the appendix), but here it will be enough to quote a few sentences that illustrate how it put our criteria to use. Let's start with the most important: apostolicity.

### Reason 1: Apostolicity

Apostolicity is a complicated word with a simple meaning. Quite straightforwardly, it points to a document's having been written either by an apostle of Jesus or by a close companion of an apostle of Jesus. Over and over again, the author of the Muratorian Canon relies on that test in particular to defend canonical books. So he says, for example, "The fourth of the Gospels was written by John, one of the disciples." Of the Gospel of Luke, he says that it was written "on Paul's authority by Luke," and similarly he says of Paul's letters that "the blessed apostle Paul himself . . . writes . . . by name to seven churches."[5]

Apostolicity was by far the most important criterion the early church used to identify and defend canonicity. The idea was profoundly simple and powerful: Not just anyone could write a book about Jesus and expect the church to recognize it as holy Scripture. No, that level of authority was reserved for those whom Jesus himself had specifically appointed apostles and for a select few close companions of the apostles.

One interesting thing to notice here is how so many would-be Scripture authors in the second through sixth centuries tried to fool the church by *slapping the names of apostles and other first-century followers of Jesus onto their documents*! Why did they do that? Simple: they knew they didn't have a chance in the world of being recognized as authoritative unless they could pass off their books as originating with an apostle or an apostolic companion.

---

[5] Quoted in Wegner, *Journey*, 147, and in J. Stevenson, ed., *A New Eusebius: Documents Illustrating the History of the Church to AD 337*, 3rd ed., rev. W. H. C. Frend (Grand Rapids, MI: Baker Academic, 2013), 137–38.

### Reason 2: Antiquity

The criterion of antiquity was closely related to that of apostolicity and, in fact, was probably used primarily to help determine whether a book was indeed apostolic. To put it simply, in order for a book to have an apostle's authority, it would have to be old, dating to the first century. Books written more recently than that simply didn't qualify because the apostles were all dead by the turn of the second century. Antiquity, therefore, didn't *assure* canonicity, but a lack of antiquity immediately *prevented* it.

This is exactly what we see in the Muratorian Canon, which rejects a book called *The Shepherd of Hermas* because it "was written quite lately in our times in the city of Rome by Hermas . . . and therefore . . . it cannot to the end of time be publicly read in the church to the people, either among the prophets, who are complete in number, or among the Apostles."[6] Newbies, the early Christians said, need not apply!

### Reason 3: Orthodoxy

The third criterion of canonization was that a book had to be in agreement with the standard of truth reflected in the doctrinal tradition handed down from Jesus himself. At first, much of that tradition was oral, passed down through the years by word of mouth. But as time passed and various Gospels and epistles were written and subsequently received as authoritative, the canon itself became the standard against which other books were measured. Thus, if a book showed up teaching

---

[6] Quoted in Wegner, *Journey*, 148; Stevenson, *New Eusebius*, 138.

something contrary to the already-recognized authoritative books, it was rejected. So the author of the Muratorian Canon says of the four Gospels, "Though various ideas are taught in the several books of the Gospels, it makes no difference to the faith of believers, since by one sovereign Spirit all things are declared in all of them concerning the Nativity, the Passion, the Resurrection, the conversation with his disciples, [and] his two comings."[7] Not only were the four Gospels apostolic and old; they were also consistent with the standard of truth and therefore to be received as authoritative without hesitation.

### Reason 4: Universality

One more criterion proved important in the early church's defense of its received canon: universality. This idea held that the only books recognized as authoritative were those that Christians in every part of the known world used and valued. If a book rose out of a specific sect or was only used in one particular part of the world, that book was rejected. On the other hand, a book that was questioned for some reason could find its case greatly strengthened if it was being used by Christians all over the world. Indeed, the widespread use of both Hebrews and Revelation contributed to both these books finally being recognized as canonical.

## So . . . Do We Have the Right Books?

Okay, so where does all this leave us? Well, it leaves us first of all with the firm conclusion that the New Testament canon

---

[7] Quoted in Wegner, *Journey*, 147; Stevenson, *New Eusebius*, 137.

resulted not from some nefarious, late-in-the-day conspiracy to privilege one set of books and suppress others that would have given us "a different perspective" on Jesus. The fact is, there weren't any such "others," not until much later, and only then as a reactive challenge to an established and increasingly strong tradition. It also leaves us with good confidence that the early Christians didn't simply appeal to mysticism or random-ness or a vague feeling of *truthiness*, as we say today, to defend their canon. On the contrary, they had good, plausible, even historically meaningful reasons for explaining why *these* books as opposed to any others were the best ones for preserving the life and teachings of Jesus: they were apostolic (and therefore ancient as well), they stood in agreement with the truth as it had been handed down for generations, and Christians the world over valued them and recognized them as authoritative.

So when it comes to the question, "Do we have the right books?" think of it like this: not one of the documents that make up our New Testament ultimately failed any of these very reasonable tests. Sure, a handful of our books took a while longer to satisfy the tests than others, but in the end, the church recognized each and every one of them as having fully and completely satisfied the criteria for authoritativeness. That means, significantly, that no book in our New Testament canon *shouldn't* be there, according to reasonable criteria. They are all ancient, all apostolic, all in agreement with the in-herited standard of truth, and all widely recognized. They are, in a word, reliable witnesses to the life and teachings of Jesus.

Moreover—and perhaps more importantly—no document

has existed in the entire history of the world that *belongs* in the canon but is not in it. Sure, some books raised eyebrows in the early centuries of the church, but in the end, each and every one of them was judged not to have been ancient, apostolic, orthodox, or widely recognized—or some combination of those. We've already seen, for example, that *The Shepherd of Hermas* failed at the point of antiquity and therefore also apostolicity. Because it was written by Hermas and not an apostle or a close companion of an apostle, the early Christians said, it couldn't be part of the authoritative canon. *The Gospel of Peter*, along with several other books, failed at two points: (1) it purported to reveal things that Jesus taught "in secret"—things that contradicted what everyone knew about what Jesus had taught quite publicly—thus failing the test of orthodoxy; and (2) it was used only in isolated and scattered parts of the church, thus failing the test of universality. And perhaps most famously, *The Gospel of Thomas* was finally rejected as authoritative not only because it was not likely written in its final form until well into the second century (which means it wasn't written by the apostle Thomas, who was truly dead by then) but also because it contained teachings that everyone knew were foreign, and even contrary, to Jesus's already well-known public teachings.

Let me put the point like this: What if you had a blank slate, an opportunity to build your own New Testament canon? How would you go about defining a list of ancient documents that should be trusted, as opposed to those that shouldn't? Do you really think you could come up with any better criteria than something like, "In order to be trusted, a book

1. needs to be written or authorized by those who were closest to Jesus (antiquity and apostolicity);
2. needs to not depart jarringly from what we've always known to be Jesus's teaching (orthodoxy); and
3. needs to not be sectarian or provincial but rather used widely among broad swaths of Christians (universality)"?

Frankly, I think coming up with something better than that would be exceedingly difficult.

To press the point, exactly which books in our current New Testament would you exclude from your new canon of "books to be trusted," and how much difference would that make to the body of Christian doctrine? Even more, which *other* books would you insist *must* be included? Would you push for *The Shepherd of Hermas*, even though most early Christians knew that it was written by a random guy over a century after Jesus's death? Would you insist on *The Gospel of Peter*, which wasn't written by Peter and is an obvious attempt to slip in "secret" teachings of Jesus that no one had ever heard of before (wink, wink, trust me, he really did say this)? Or how about *The Gospel of Thomas*, which wasn't written by Thomas and would require you to canonize passages like this:

> Simon Peter said to them, "Let Mary leave us, for women are not worthy of Life."
>
> Jesus said, "I myself shall lead her in order to make her male, so that she too may become a living spirit resem-

bling you males. For every woman who will make herself
male will enter the Kingdom of Heaven."[8]

(Yes, it really says that.) You see the point? If we're honest in
light of all this, I doubt any of us would finally come up with
a better collection of to-be-trusted documents than the early
church did.

In fact, when you think about it, the early Christians seem
to have done a pretty good job identifying which documents
should be considered trustworthy guides to what Jesus actually
said and did. On the one hand, it doesn't at all seem that they
engaged in some power-play conspiracy to suppress perfectly
good *other* documents. And on the other hand, the documents
they *did* defend as authoritative seem to have pretty solid reasons arguing in their favor.

If all that's the case, then we don't need to fear that we've
somehow got the wrong documents—that is, that there are
actually others out there somewhere that would give us a *better*
picture of who Jesus is and what he did than the New Testament. In fact, we can have a great deal of confidence that the
books we have are indeed the *best* ones—the most ancient, the
most trustworthy, the most, in a word, reliable.

Of course, that only matters for our purposes if the writers of these documents really were trying to convey accurate
information.

But what if they weren't?

---

[8] *The Gospel of Thomas*, saying 114; English translation quoted in Blomberg, *Can We Still
Believe the Bible?*, 73.

# 5

# But Can I Trust You?

"Streets are all jammed. Noise in crowds like New Year's Eve in city. Wait a minute . . . Enemy now in sight above the Palisades. Five—five great machines. First one is crossing river. I can see it from here . . . A bulletin's handed me . . . Martian cylinders are falling all over the country. One outside Buffalo, one in Chicago, St. Louis . . . seem to be timed and spaced . . . Now the first machine reaches the shore. He stands watching, looking over the city . . . He waits for the others. They rise like a line of new towers on the city's west side . . . Now they're lifting their metal hands. *This is the end now.* Smoke comes out . . . black smoke, drifting over the city. People in the streets see it now! They're running towards the East River . . . thousands of them, dropping in like rats! Now the smoke's spreading faster. It's reached Times Square. People trying to run away from it, but it's no use. They're falling like flies! Now the smoke's crossing Sixth Avenue . . . Fifth Avenue . . . one hundred yards away . . . it's fifty feet . . ."

[Then the sound of choking, then a struggle, then silence. And then this, crackling over the airwaves:] "2X2L calling CQ . . . 2X2L calling CQ . . . New York? Isn't there anyone on the air? Isn't there anyone on the air? Isn't there anyone . . ."[1]

On Sunday, October 30, 1938, at about 8:15 in the evening, that's the news broadcast that people all over the country heard as they tuned into the Columbia Broadcasting System (CBS). Within minutes, the station's New York–based producer was on the phone with an irate Midwestern mayor demanding that the station cease its broadcast because mobs had begun crowding the streets of his town. Soon after that, reporters from other news outlets poured into CBS's headquarters, demanding answers. Here's how the producer described the scene:

The following hours were a nightmare. The building was suddenly full of people and dark-blue uniforms. . . . Finally the Press was let loose upon us, ravening for horror. How many deaths had *we* heard of? (Implying they knew of thousands.) What did *we* know of the fatal stampede in a Jersey hall? (Implying it was one of many.) What traffic deaths? (The ditches must be choked with corpses.) The suicides? (Haven't you heard about the one on Riverside Drive?) It is all quite vague in my memory and quite terrible.[2]

---

[1] "The War of the Worlds," Internet Sacred Text Archive, accessed May 26, 2015, http://www.sacred-texts.com/ufo/mars/wow.htm.

[2] John Houseman, *Run Through: A Memoir* (New York: Simon & Schuster, 1972), 404.

It turns out that, thank goodness, there weren't actually any deaths at all that night—either from stampedes, or traffic, or suicide. Nor were there any at the hands of Martians. That's because the "news broadcast" that reportedly sent so many people into a panic that day was actually just a radio show, a dramatic production of H. G. Wells's novel *The War of the Worlds.*

People have always wondered what led folks to panic over a radio show. I mean, they had heard fictionalized dramas before; indeed, "The War of the Worlds" was part of a series called *The Mercury Theatre on Air.* But in this case, several factors—fears about looming war with Germany, the fact that commercial breaks were spaced farther apart in this show than usual, several listeners missing the opening because a popular program on another channel ran long—created a perfect storm that made a good number of people *really think that Martians were invading New York City*!

It's fascinating to compare that episode with the accounts of Jesus's life in the Bible. What if, like many of the people who listened to CBS's broadcast of "The War of the Worlds," we're simply misunderstanding the biblical writers' purpose? What if they weren't really trying to tell us what was actually happening but rather doing something else—perhaps writing fiction, creating legend, or even trying to deceive? In other words, given that we can now be very confident

1. that our translations of the biblical manuscripts are reliable,
2. that our biblical manuscripts accurately reflect what the originals said, and

3. that we are, in fact, looking at the right and best documents for getting information,

the next question is, can we be confident that the people who wrote the biblical documents were themselves *trustworthy*? Were they actually intending to tell us accurately what they believed had happened?[3]

## Searching for Clues

The interesting thing about the "War of the Worlds" fiasco is that over and over throughout the program, the broadcasters gave clues that what you were listening to was not a real news report but a fictionalized drama. They weren't subtle clues either. For example, the very first words that came over the airwaves were, "The Columbia Broadcasting System and its affiliated stations present Orson Welles and the Mercury Theatre on the Air in *The War of the Worlds* by H. G. Wells."[4] Also, the very next words after the guy choked on the Martian gas were, "You are listening to a CBS presentation of Orson Welles and The Mercury Theatre on the Air in an original dramatization of *The War of the Worlds* by H. G. Wells. The performance will continue after a brief intermission."[5] The program broke for commercials four times during the broadcast. Even so, CBS was obliged to make an announcement *three more times* that evening *over its entire nationwide network* that Mars had not actually attacked!

---

[3] For this chapter, I have relied especially on Craig L. Blomberg, *The Historical Reliability of the Gospels,* 2nd ed. (Downers Grove, IL: IVP Academic, 2007).
[4] "War of the Worlds."
[5] Ibid.

For those listeners who tuned in to Orson Welles's "Mercury Theatre on the Air" broadcast from 8 to 9 p.m. Eastern Standard Time tonight and did not realize that the program was merely a modernized adaptation of H. G. Wells's famous novel *War of the Worlds*, we are repeating the fact which was made clear four times on the program, that, while the names of some American cities were used, as in all novels and dramatizations, the entire story and all of its incidents were fictitious.[6]

For crying out loud—and this was CBS's point in that snarky last announcement—people should have heard the clues! They should have picked up on the indications in the program itself that it wasn't actually intending to report real events. Everything was right there in front them.

Alright, so to return to our question, we need to ask now whether the Bible gives any clues like that. Does it give any indication that we should read the whole thing *not* as an attempt at history but rather as fiction or legend or myth or something else? Well, the Bible does indeed give some clues, but they actually point in the *other* direction. They all point to the conclusion that the biblical writers *were* in fact intending to report events accurately as they saw them.

## What Were They Doing?

Here's the thing. If you want to assert that the biblical writers had a different intent than accurate reporting, intellectual

[6] Hadley Cantril, Hazel Gaudet, and Herta Herzog, *The Invasion from Mars: A Study in the Psychology of Panic, with the Complete Script of the Famous Orson Welles Broadcast* (Princeton, NJ: Princeton University Press, 1940), 43–44.

honesty demands not that you just *assert* such a claim but that you propose a plausible alternative. If they weren't trying to report events accurately, then what exactly were they doing? Let's think about it:

1. The biblical authors might have had a *nonhistorical purpose* in writing. Perhaps they, like H. G. Wells, were just writing a novel of sorts, which they knew wasn't true and which they never intended anyone else to take as true either. Similarly, perhaps they were constructing a legend—that is, taking a set of fairly unremarkable events and embellishing them with extraordinary details. True, people who develop legends very often believe that their stories can say something—however cryptically—about reality or their people's origins, even as they also know that the outlandish details of the story are made up. Of course, the trouble is that subsequent listeners and readers don't always make the distinction and just think the whole story is true. So maybe what we have in the Bible is *fiction* or *legend*, not reporting, and Christians just aren't getting the gag.

2. The biblical authors might have had a *deceitful purpose*. Perhaps they, like so many people before and after them, were intentionally trying to pull the wool over everyone's eyes and get them to believe something that never really happened. Maybe it was all a giant hoax, a power play, or ambition run amok.

3. The biblical authors themselves *might have been deceived*. You wouldn't have to think that someone deliberately deceived them to say that. Perhaps their own minds deceived

them, or perhaps the traditions they heard from other Christians had been corrupted. Whatever it was, maybe the authors *unwittingly* passed the deception on to us.

4. Finally, it might not matter much what the biblical authors purposed to do, because even if they *were* trying to give us accurate descriptions of what happened, their accounts are so *hopelessly confused, contradictory, and error ridden* that we finally can't trust anything about them.

Maybe one of these scenarios actually captures reality. But what if we could be confident that none of them does? If it becomes probable that the authors were *not* intending to write fiction or legend, that they were *not* trying to deceive, that they were *not* deluded or deceived themselves, and that their writings are *not* error ridden as some have charged, then we could conclude with a high degree of confidence that the authors indeed *intended* to give us accurate information, at which point we could confidently say, "Those documents are *historically reliable*." Now that's not to say yet that we can be confident they finally got it right; that's a question for the next chapter. But it still gets us a long way, because it's no small thing to be able to say with confidence, "The biblical authors weren't writing fiction, they weren't perpetrating a hoax, they weren't deluded, and they weren't hopelessly confused. They really believed all this happened."

## Writers of Fiction?

Let's start thinking through this matter by considering the first possibility, that the biblical authors might have had a *nonhistorical purpose* and that they didn't intend for us actually to *believe* what they were saying. The first question to ask here is whether the authors perhaps told us straight-out somewhere that they were writing fiction, kind of like CBS telling their listeners that they were listening to a drama. The answer is no. The Bible contains nothing at all like this. In fact, over and over again the biblical authors quite plainly state the opposite. They tell us, as clearly as words will allow, that they really do believe what they're saying, and they want us to believe it too.

Here, for example, is how Luke begins his account of Jesus's life:

> Inasmuch as many have undertaken to compile a narrative of the things that have been accomplished among us, just as those who from the beginning were eyewitnesses and ministers of the word have delivered them to us, it seemed good to me also, having followed all things closely for some time past, to write an orderly account for you, most excellent Theophilus, that you may have certainty concerning the things you have been taught. (Luke 1:1–4)

How could he be any clearer about his intention? Luke has "followed all things closely for some time," and now he is writing "an orderly account" of those things so that this fellow Theophilus "may have certainty concerning the things" he has been taught about Jesus. Whatever Luke is doing, he's not writing a story just for our enjoyment; he wants us to believe his account with certainty.

John too tells us his intention for writing an account of Jesus's life:

> Now Jesus did many other signs in the presence of the disciples, which are not written in this book; but these are written so that you may believe that Jesus is the Christ, the Son of God, and that by believing you may have life in his name. (John 20:30–31)

See? Again, he's not writing fiction; he really wants people to believe that Jesus is the Christ, which means that he wants us to believe that the things he wrote in his book really happened.

In another place too, John tells us his intention for writing:

> That which was from the beginning, which we have heard, which we have seen with our eyes, which we looked upon and have touched with our hands . . . that which we have seen and heard we proclaim also to you. (1 John 1:1, 3)

Do you see? The last thing John intends for anyone to say in response to his books is, "Oh, that John, what a good storyteller. He really should get a book contract!" No, he wants us to know that he actually and truly and really saw some things, heard them, even *touched* them and experienced them, and now he's proclaiming them to us. At least as far as his stated intention, John isn't writing fiction or legend; he really wants us to believe what he's saying.

Beyond these obvious statements of intention, the biblical authors give other indications that they want us to believe what they're writing. For example, think about how often the authors refer to specific, verifiable historical events and circumstances. Such allusions pepper the New Testament, but one example ought to make the point. Look at this short passage from Luke's Gospel:

> In the fifteenth year of the reign of Tiberius Caesar, Pontius Pilate being governor of Judea, and Herod being tetrarch of Galilee, and his brother Philip tetrarch of the region of Ituraea and Trachonitis, and Lysanias tetrarch of Abilene, during the high priesthood of Annas and Caiaphas, the word of God came to John the son of Zechariah in the wilderness. (3:1–2)

One author has pointed out that in the space of just two verses here, Luke packs no fewer than twenty-one references to historical people, places, and circumstances, each and every one of which is (and would have been as soon as Luke wrote them) testable and verifiable—or *falsifiable* if Luke got them wrong![7] We find Luke's same attention to detail in his second book, Acts, and the other authors of the New Testament likewise include contemporary, verifiable references in their writings. Here's the point again: Luke and the other biblical authors weren't writing fiction or legend; rather, they were careful to weave their stories into the verifiable, detailed tapestry of real, historical life. They genuinely wanted us to believe what they wrote.

---

[7] Nathan Busenitz, *Reasons We Believe: 50 Lines of Evidence That Confirm the Christian Faith* (Wheaton, IL: Crossway, 2008), 127.

But what if they just genuinely wanted us to believe the lies they were telling?

## With Deceitful Intent?

That brings us to the second possibility, that the biblical authors might have had a *deceitful purpose*. Couldn't it be that they were just perpetrating a hoax on the world, trying to get us to believe things that didn't actually happen? Isn't it possible that, while they repeatedly insisted they were telling the truth—even throwing in historical facts for good measure—they were really just reeling us in to dupe us and make us believe a bunch of lies?

Well, sure. Anything's possible. But our goal here isn't to identify something that's *barely possible*. It's to try to come to some kind of confidence about what is *probable*. And the fact is, when you think about the situation carefully, the probability that the biblical authors were trying to deceive us drops to about as close to absolute zero as we can possibly get. Let's think about a few points.

First of all, pulling off a gigantic hoax of this kind would have been exceedingly difficult, if not impossible. For one thing, all twenty-seven books of the New Testament were written within just a few decades of Jesus's life. That means that as those books were beginning to circulate, literally hundreds—and probably even thousands—of people were still alive who had seen Jesus and what he did with their own eyes. So if Luke, for example, was just making things up or even embellishing them, plenty of people around could have said, "Hold up. That didn't happen. You're fabricating your story, Luke." We have no record of anyone ever saying that. This point becomes even stronger when you realize that even the people who had the biggest stake in putting an end to Christianity didn't *deny* that Jesus really did and said the things the biblical authors claimed he did. They simply accused him of being a liar or being wrong. If there had been any reason to think that he *hadn't* said them—that the biblical authors had simply made it all up—you can bet the opponents of Christianity would have wasted no time pointing that out.

Second, not only would pulling off a deception of that magnitude in the presence of so many eyewitnesses have been exceedingly difficult, but if anyone *was* trying to do that, the guys they settled on as their primary spokesmen were not very obvious choices. Think about it. Did you know that two of the four authors of the Gospels—Luke and Mark—were not apostles of Jesus, nor did either of them ever lay eyes on him? Luke was a close friend and travel companion of Paul, but he was far from a prominent leader in the church and had no inherent claim to any authority. John Mark was a friend and companion of both Peter and Paul, but he is actually best known for abandoning Paul in Pamphylia and then having Paul reject him in a "sharp disagreement" when he wanted to rejoin the work (Acts 13:13; 15:37–41)! Even Matthew, though he was indeed one of the apostles, had been a turncoat tax collector for the Romans. Now if you were trying to deceive the world with a hoax, it's hard to imagine that your first draft picks would be a relative nobody, a divisive deserter, and a tax man. That wouldn't exactly set you up for success.

This brings us to a third point. If the writers of the New Testament were trying to deceive the world or pull off a hoax, what plausible motive could they possibly have had? To make a name for themselves? To get rich? To become powerful leaders in a powerful church? If that was their plan, then we have to say that they failed spectacularly. Most of the apostles wound up being killed, whether by having their heads chopped off, being crucified, or enduring other gruesome methods of execution.

On top of that, if their motive was in some way to make themselves look good—or even to lie or exaggerate in order to make *Christianity* look good—then they sabotaged themselves by including way too many embarrassing details, including things that make the heroes of the story look, well, less than heroic. If you're trying to pull off a hoax to make your new religion attractive, why would you keep pointing out how your future leaders were as dense as rocks when it came to understanding what Jesus was saying? Why would you include the story about Peter misunderstanding Jesus so badly that he cut off a guy's ear, only to get scolded like an errant child? For that matter, why would you tell strange stories about Jesus (this omniscient God-man you're trying to invent), not knowing who it was that touched his cloak or crying with a couple of women in front of a tomb or peevishly cursing a fig tree to death because it didn't have anything for him to eat?

Yes, I know that Christians say all those stories ultimately have a profound meaning behind them (and they do), but any Christian preacher will admit that it takes some *work* to get there—that meaning is not right on the surface. And therein lies the point: If you were concocting a hoax with the motive of making your new religion, its founder, and its leaders look good, those are not the kinds of stories you would invent. And you certainly wouldn't air out your dirty laundry by telling the story of how Mark deserted Paul, Paul rejected Mark when he returned, and the whole thing caused a gigantic falling out. The only reason you tell those stories and air all that dirty laundry is not to make the whole thing look good but to *tell it like it happened.*

Of course, you can always go all *Manchurian Candidate* on us and say that all those embarrassing details were just put there to knock us off the trail, to make us *think* they were telling it like it was, when actually they were lying to us. But at that point you would be several layers deep into a conspiracy theory, and it would be fair to wonder if your aim was really to arrive at the truth or just defend your presuppositions.

Anyway, let me make one more point here, one that applies to everything we've said so far in this chapter. Nobody dies for a fiction, and nobody dies for a hoax. If your goal in writing something was simply to write a novel or to perpetrate a deception, you don't stick to the story once the jig is up and your head is about to come off. The only way you stick to the story under those circumstances is if you *really believe that what you wrote actually happened.* And that's exactly what we have in the people who wrote the New Testament. Even as they wrote and taught, they knew they could be killed for what they were saying. And yet through all the threats and all the promises, even up to the moment of their own deaths, *they kept on saying it.* Slice it however you like. These guys were not writing fiction, and they were not lying. They believed what they wrote, and they wanted us to believe it too.

## Simply Duped?

But there's another possibility, isn't there? What if the biblical authors were not so much deceivers as deceived themselves? That theory has been suggested in several different forms through the centuries, but it never really ends up holding much water. One famous version of it, for example, accuses all the disciples of having a mass hallucination of a risen Jesus and then going back and writing legends to fill in a backstory. But it doesn't take much thought to realize how unlikely that is. "Mass hallucination" is a nonsensical idea to begin with. By definition, hallucinations are internal, personal, and individual. They happen in an individual person's mind, and unless you want to posit some kind of ESP or paranormal mental connection between humans, they are therefore not contagious. Besides, given how many different groups of people reported seeing Jesus, how many different times, and over how many weeks, the notion of a sustained, contagious mass hallucination begins to border on the ridiculous.

Another more sophisticated version of this theory holds that Jesus's disciples were suffering from a kind of pathological wishful thinking. Unable to accept the reality of Jesus's death, the argument goes, they lived in a fantasy world of believing and claiming that he was actually alive and then wrote legends to create a backstory. Despite its more sophisticated packaging, the idea that the disciples were suffering from pathological wishful thinking is about as plausible as mass hallucination. That's because, regardless of anything else, there's no way the disciples would have been *wishing* for Jesus to be resurrected. Even if they were broken up, unable to come to terms with his death, and casting about for some way to continue thinking he was still alive, they would never have lit upon the idea of *resurrection* to comfort themselves. Why not? Because to the first-century Jews, resurrection was a theological concept with a very specific meaning: it was an event that would happen *only* at the end of time when all the dead would be raised *together*, some to be condemned by God and others to be glorified. *Nothing* in all the history of thought and religion would have planted in the disciples' minds an idea that one man might experience that resurrection and glorification *early*. Really, this "wishful thinking" charge would make much more sense if the disciples had claimed that Jesus was simply *spiritually* alive or that he had not truly died or even that he had been resuscitated from death (like Lazarus). But what they actually claimed—that Jesus had gone *through* death and come out the other side alive—was something new and completely unprecedented. That kind of idea—one that requires you to recalibrate your entire worldview—doesn't just pop into your mind as a result of *wishing*; it grows slowly and takes root when the things you've seen and experienced have rendered every other explanation utterly implausible.

Besides that, a gullible, naïve, wishful-thinking-like willingness to believe that Jesus was alive is pretty much exactly the opposite of how the biblical writers describe the disciples. Matthew reports that "some doubted" (Matt. 28:17), and Luke says that when the women came to tell them that Jesus was alive, "these words seemed to them an idle tale, and they did not believe them" (Luke 24:11). Even when Jesus appeared to the disciples, Luke says, "they were startled and frightened and thought they saw a spirit" (Luke 24:37). And then there's Thomas, who refused to believe until he could place his finger into the mark of the nails and his hand in Jesus's side (John 20:24–25).

None of this skepticism (to anticipate a counterargument) is held out in the Bible as a virtue, as if the authors were saying, "Look at these strong-minded, not-gullible-at-all men. Surely *they of all people* wouldn't have believed Jesus was alive unless it really happened!" On the contrary, the Bible portrays the disciples' unbelief as a significant embarrassment. Jesus more than once rebukes them for it, and he even tells Thomas, essentially, "You have believed because you have seen me. But blessed are those who believe *without seeing*!" Do you see the point? By highlighting the disciples' failure to believe, the Bible isn't holding them up as exemplars of hard-nosed, evidence-driven skepticism. It's telling us what happened, even if it's embarrassing, and what happened was emphatically not a case of pathological wishful thinking.

One final version of this self-deceived argument is that the oral tradition on which the biblical authors sometimes relied to write their books *must have* gotten corrupted through the years. After all, Jesus died in AD 33 and the earliest New

Testament Gospel wasn't written until around AD 60. Are we really supposed to think that the teachings of and stories about Jesus could survive intact, uncorrupted, and without addition or subtraction, through *twenty-seven whole years* of being transmitted solely by word of mouth? Again, we must mention a few things here. First of all, though all the New Testament writers seem to have used oral traditions to some degree, you have to remember that most of them—Matthew, John, Peter, James, and Jude—were eyewitnesses to the whole thing. If the oral tradition had been corrupted, they would have known it. Not only that, but when you combine Jesus's claim that his teaching held as much authority as the Old Testament prophets with the fact that a huge portion of his teaching was preserved in pithy, easy-to-remember forms, it's not surprising at all that the early Christians would be both able and determined to remember and recite it word-for-word for a very long time.

On top of all that, when it comes to oral transmission, you just have to realize that twenty-seven years is simply not very long at all for a tradition to remain intact. Let's do an experiment. Recite the nursery rhyme "Jack and Jill." I'm serious. Go ahead; do it. It doesn't have to be out loud, but at least in your mind, run through all the words of "Jack and Jill." Now, my guess is that you probably said something like this:

> Jack and Jill
> Went up the hill
> To fetch a pail of water;
> Jack fell down

And broke his crown,
And Jill came tumbling after.

Do you know when "Jack and Jill" was written? No, you don't. Nobody does, though there is still considerable debate about that question! As far as we know, the earliest *surviving* publication of the rhyme comes from a book called *Mother Goose's Melody: or, Sonnets for the Cradle*, printed in London in 1791, well over two hundred years ago.[8] Now here's the thing: Have you ever seen that book? Did you learn "Jack and Jill" by reading it in the 1791 edition of *Mother Goose's Melody?* I bet you didn't; in fact, I bet you didn't look it up in *any* book at all. I bet someone just *taught* you to recite it at some point. Moreover, I bet the person who taught you "Jack and Jill" didn't look it up in the 1791 book or any other book either. Someone likely taught it to him or her, and that someone was taught by someone else, who was taught by someone else, who was taught by yet someone else, for a very long time. That's an oral tradition. So, how much do you imagine the past two hundred-plus years of largely oral transmission has acted to corrupt and change "Jack and Jill"? How much would you guess our modern version differs from the one published in 1791? Take a look:

*Jack* and *Gill*
Went up the hill,

---

[8] A facsimile of the 1791 edition of *Mother Goose's Melody* can be found in Colonel W. F. Prideaux, ed., *Mother Goose's Melody: A Facsimile Reproduction of the Earliest Known Edition, with an Introduction and Notes* (London: A. H. Bullen, 1904), available online at Internet Archive, accessed May 26, 2015, https://archive.org/stream/mothergoosesmelo00 pridiala#page/n27/mode/2up.

To fetch a pail of water;
*Jack* fell down
And broke his crown,
And *Gill* came tumbling after.[9]

That's it. That's how it was printed, complete with italics, in 1791! With the exception of spelling "Gill" with a *J* now, the way we recite the poem "Jack and Jill" is the same today as it was *over two hundred years ago*. So let me say it again: holding things intact through a mere twenty-seven years of oral transmission just wouldn't be all that hard.

Look, the point here isn't that "Jack and Jill" is precisely parallel to the New Testament oral tradition; it's not, and you can probably identify many differences between the two. The point is simply that maintaining an oral tradition over even a very long time is not as difficult as it might seem to us, much less impossible.

So here's where we are: none of the various versions of the "deceived authors" theory finally hold any water. The charge that the disciples experienced a mass hallucination isn't plausible and doesn't make any sense anyway. Nor do the disciples seem to have been suffering a pathological case of wishful thinking. And finally, as eyewitnesses themselves of the actual events, they certainly weren't the unwitting victims of a corrupted oral tradition only twenty-seven years old.

---

[9] Prideaux, *Mother Goose's Melody*, 37, https://archive.org/stream/mothergoosesmelo00 pridiala#page/37/mode/2up.

## Utterly Confused?

The authors of the New Testament documents were not writing fiction, they were not trying to deceive, and they were not themselves deluded or deceived. One final possibility remains, though, and that is that the writers' purpose ultimately does not matter. And the reason it doesn't matter is because, even if they *were* trying to give us accurate descriptions of what happened, their books are so hopelessly confused, contradictory, and error ridden that we finally can't trust anything about them.

Perhaps the most important thing to say in response to this charge is that it's a misconception held by many who *haven't* looked at the evidence and by almost none who *have*. That's because, even though the Bible has been subjected to scorching and detailed assault by skeptics for more than two hundred years, it's reasonable to say that every alleged contradiction, inconsistency, and error has been met with at least one plausible resolution and often more. I realize that's a sweeping and gigantic assertion, and the best way to prove it would be to spend hundreds of pages creating a compendium of alleged "problem points" and then analyzing them to see if there are plausible resolutions. We're actually not going to do that kind of gritty, exhaustive work here, though, because other books have done it many times over. Therefore, if some particular place in the Bible has stumped you, I would encourage you to seek out one of those books, look up the problem, and read about it (see appendix). With patient study and careful understanding, even the most intractable problems will give way.

On the other hand, if you're a person who actually *makes* this charge against the Bible, then I'll put it to you as straight as I can: I think you have an intellectual responsibility either to stop making that charge or actually to read Christian scholars' good-faith efforts to bring plausible—usually even *probable*—resolutions to the inconsistencies and errors that skeptics have alleged. All that work may not finally and fully convince you, I know. You may walk away still scratching your head or even crowing about a few passages, and that's fine. I can assure you, though, that if you do that work, you'll walk away with more convincing answers than unconvincing ones. What you simply *can't* do, though—not with any intellectual integrity, at least— is just go on insisting that the Bible is hopelessly contradictory and error ridden but at the same time refuse to do the work necessary to test that assertion. So check it out. You might be surprised at what you find.

The fact is, a whole lot of the inconsistencies alleged by skeptics turn out *not* to be problematic at all when you read them a little more carefully. Despite two centuries of nit-picking, scholars have proposed plausible resolutions to *every single one* of the alleged inconsistencies. You just need sufficient intellectual integrity to take the time to look them up in a book.

But let's say you're unconvinced by any of the explanations, even after you study them carefully. You still have to ask yourself, "Do the apparent discrepancies in the accounts sufficiently prove that *nothing happened* or that we *can't know anything* about what happened?" I mean, how much sense would it make, really, to say, "Wow, Matthew says there were *two* women at the empty tomb of Jesus, while Luke says there were *three or more* women at his empty tomb. Clearly, we can't know anything at all about what happened on that Sunday morning." Of course you wouldn't say that! Pointing out a few apparent discrepancies of detail in the accounts of eyewitnesses might mean a lot of things, but it certainly doesn't mean that *nothing happened*—nor does it mean that we can't know anything about what happened.

While we're at it, this very question—about how many women were at the tomb—provides a good example of how we can easily harmonize *apparent* inconsistencies. Matthew doesn't claim that *only* two women went; he simply mentions only two women by name (Matt. 28:1). And Luke doesn't say anything about how many women went to the tomb but rather says that three women whom he names, as well as some "other women," told the apostles about what happened at the tomb (Luke 24:10). So what's going on here? Are Matthew and Luke contradicting one another? No, if you just think about it a bit, there are a number of possible resolutions. Perhaps Luke simply offers a more comprehensive picture of the number of women who went to the tomb than Matthew does, while Matthew only names two particular women out of the larger group. Or it's also possible that indeed only two women went to the tomb, but when they returned they told other women, and then the whole lot of them reported the story to the disciples. Either way, you get the point: we can rehearse many plausible resolutions to apparent inconsistencies, and we shouldn't be too quick to cry, "Contradiction!"

Even beyond that, historically speaking, the fact that the narratives haven't had all their apparent discrepancies corrected and brought into line actually speaks well of their reliability. As one scholar puts it,

> The stories exhibit . . . exactly that surface tension which we associate, not with tales artfully told by people eager to sustain a fiction and therefore anxious to make everything look right, but with the hurried, puzzled accounts of those who have seen with their own eyes something which took them by surprise and with which they have not yet fully come to terms.[10]

In the end, it's perfectly reasonable to conclude that the biblical documents are not nearly as contradictory, confused, and error ridden as uninformed people assume. And even where the details of particular stories *don't* immediately line up, that evidence hardly forces us to throw up our hands and declare that nothing happened. In fact, it gives the accounts of Jesus's life exactly the kind of character we would expect them to have if several witnesses to an extraordinary set of events sat down, not to tell fiction, not to deceive, not to perpetrate a hoax, but simply to say *what they believed happened.*

## A Big Moment

Okay, this is an important moment. So take a deep breath and reengage! At this point in the argument, we can draw an im-

---

[10] N. T. Wright, *The Resurrection of the Son of God*, vol. 3 of *Christian Origins and the Question of God* (Minneapolis: Fortress, 2003), 612.

mensely significant conclusion. We can say with a very high degree of confidence that . . . wait for it . . .

The Bible is historically reliable.

Do you remember how we got here? Moving from ourselves as readers back through time toward the events recorded, we've determined that we can be very confident that

1. our translations of the biblical manuscripts are accurate;
2. our biblical manuscripts accurately reflect what the originals said;
3. we are, in fact, looking at the right and best documents for getting information; and
4. the authors of the biblical documents were not writing fiction, were not deceiving, and were not themselves deluded or deceived, but were actually writing to tell us what they believed happened.

If those four statements really.are reasonable conclusions, then we can trust the Bible to tell us what the writers actually believed had happened.

Of course, that leaves us with one final question: Can we have any confidence that what the writers *believed* happened . . . really did happen?

# 6

# So Did It Happen?

I probably don't have to convince you that people can sometimes be very sure about something, and yet at the same time be absolutely wrong. I can't tell you how many times in my life I've been absolutely sure that I saw something happen, only to find out later that what I *thought* I saw wasn't really what happened at all.

This is the final issue we need to confront as we consider the reliability of the Bible. Is it possible that the biblical authors were *intending* to tell us what really happened, that they themselves even believed that the things they recorded really happened, and yet that they were just wrong about it? I don't mean that they were deluded or trying to pull off a hoax or writing fiction but—as we've all experienced from time to time—just flat wrong? To put the question more sharply, can we in any way know for certain that the biblical authors were in fact *right* in what they recorded—that is, that what they *thought* happened and what they *said* happened really *did* happen?[1]

---

[1] For this chapter, I have relied especially on Craig L. Blomberg, *Can We Still Believe the Bible? An Evangelical Engagement with Contemporary Questions* (Grand Rapids, MI: Brazos, 2014); N. T. Wright, *The Resurrection of the Son of God*, vol. 3 of *Christian Origins and the Question of God* (Minneapolis: Fortress, 2003).

Well, no, there's no way to know *for certain* if what you're talking about is *mathematical certainty*. But we have to remember that we're *never* able to reach mathematical certainty about historical events. Between you and every event in history that you didn't experience firsthand lies a gap that no amount of logic, reasoning, equation running, or evidence gathering will ever be able to close entirely. It will always be possible— *barely* possible, but possible nonetheless—that we are all just *wrong* about *everything*. Someone once referred to that certainty gap as a "broad and ugly ditch."[2] And a few people, staring into that ditch, have simply thrown up their hands and declared that we should never really trust any historical claim. But that extreme position would throw us into a dark, historical nihilism, and surely none of us wants to live like that—or even has the *ability* to do so consistently. No, we all know that even if we can't arrive at mathematical certainty about events in history, we can in fact arrive at *historical confidence* about them—a high enough degree of confidence to say, "Yes, I'm very sure that happened," and then even to live by, rely on, and act on those events.

History, then, doesn't trade in mathematical certainties. In fact, it doesn't even look for certainties. Instead, it looks for probabilities, which ultimately translate into confidence that something actually happened. So for any given event, history first asks whether the source who reported it seems reliable, using exactly the kinds of questions we've been asking of the

---

[2] Gotthold Ephraim Lessing, "On the Proof of the Spirit and of Power," in *Philosophical and Theological Writings*, ed. H. B. Nisbet, Cambridge Texts in the History of Philosophy (Cambridge: Cambridge University Press, 2005), 87.

Bible. Then, once it determines that the source does seem reliable, it asks, "Okay, is it plausible to think that what this reliable source has reported actually happened as an event in history?" Usually, that question can be very quickly answered with a "Yes, of course it's plausible." If a reliable source says that such and such an army crossed such and such a river, if there's nothing inherently implausible about that crossing, and if no other evidence causes us to think that maybe the army *didn't* cross the river, then we generally say, "Yes, such and such an army *did indeed* cross the river." That's not mathematical certainty, but it is *strong* historical confidence.

## The Problem of Miracles

Here's the problem, though, when it comes to the Bible. Sure, it tells stories of armies crossing rivers—but only after God splits the river in half so the army can walk on dry land! It also tells of a man instantly turning water into wine and walking on the surface of the sea and healing people with a word and even rising from the dead three days after he is killed. So what gives with all that? Well, let's be honest. When a historical source— even one we've determined to be genuinely *reliable*—starts reporting things like that, we don't greet those reports with the same yawn and "yeah, yeah" that we would give a report that an army crossed a river. We tend to greet them with, "Come on. You can't be serious!"

Why do we respond like that? Well, probably a few things factor into our natural skepticism of miracle stories, but the most obvious one is also, I think, the most important. People who are naturally skeptical of miracles are people who *haven't experienced them*. There's nothing surprising about that; we all naturally find it hard to believe things that lie completely outside our experience.

Here's one often-used example: Imagine a man who lived all his life—a long time ago, before electricity or any modern technology—on a tropical island near the equator. One day, a ship shows up, and the sailors tell him they're from a country far away in the north. Then they begin to talk about this fantastic substance called *ice*, which is like water turning into a rock when it gets very cold. Now our friend on the equatorial island has absolutely no experience of ice, nor even (likely) of the kind of cold required to make it. So probably, he's going to have a very hard time believing that this "water turning into a very cold rock" has ever actually happened. He may even declare it to be *impossible* and the sailors to be dupes or liars. Ice lies utterly and completely outside his experience, and he doesn't believe in it.

And yet ice exists.

When it comes to miracles, I think many of us are like that tropical guy with the ice. We've never experienced anyone walking on water or turning water into wine or rising from the dead, so we begin with an assumption that those things don't—indeed, *can't*—happen. But just because we've never experienced them doesn't mean they don't exist, just as it's ridiculous to say that ice doesn't exist because the island man has never seen any. In fact, for someone who *has* experienced miracles—and millions of people in the world say they have—

this whole question of whether miracles are plausible (much less possible) seems pretty silly. "Of course they're plausible," those people say; "I've *seen* them." Sure, you can be like the islander and insist that all those people are dupes or liars, but they'll just shake their heads, smile, and say, "Someday, my friend, I hope you have the pleasure of experiencing ice cream."

You see? All that is to say that you can't just declare miracles—and therefore the Bible—to be implausible simply on the strength of your own experience or lack thereof. Other people have had different experiences than yours, and to say that every experience at odds with your own is necessarily flawed would be the height of arrogance. Therefore, if you're going to declare miracles to be inherently implausible, you're going to need a reason to do so.

## Arguments against Miracles— The Scientific Objection

Over the centuries, people have offered two main arguments for declaring miracles—including the ones reported by the biblical authors—to be hopelessly implausible or even impossible. Let's take a moment to think about each of those.

First, some have offered a *scientific objection* to miracles of any kind. That objection says essentially that the advances in science particularly over the past two centuries have proven that miracles are impossible. People only believed in miracles in the first place, it's said, because they didn't understand how the world works and were therefore unduly inclined toward believing in the supernatural. They had gaps in their understanding of biology and astronomy and chemistry and ecology, and they filled them in by appealing to miracles. Today, though, because science has filled in so many of the gaps that miracles used to bridge, we can safely conclude that miracles are unnecessary and therefore that they do not really happen.

Is it really that simple, though? I mean, even the very first premise—that people only believed in miracles because they didn't understand how the world works as well as *we* do—doesn't really apply very well to most of the miracles in the Bible. After all, even the most ancient people knew very well that two people are required to make a baby, that if you try to walk on water you sink, and that dead people do not rise again! And yet the biblical writers said, "Those things happened. We saw them happen." On top of this, for all our newfound knowledge, we still can't explain the things they witnessed any better than they could. I mean, it's not as if we can now say to the biblical writers, "Hey, you simpleminded people, don't you realize that it actually wasn't a miracle at all for a man to walk on water? Had you known, as we do now, about the laws of quantum physics and the theory of relativity, you would have understood that walking on water is a completely *natural* phenomenon and nothing at all to get excited about. And neither, by the way, is a baby being born of a virgin, a man calming a storm or healing the sick with a word, or a man rising from the dead. Science can explain those too." No, the fact is, science hasn't made those events any less astonishing for us than they were for them.

You see my point? The trouble with saying that science

has advanced to the point that we can now explain miracles naturalistically—including the ones in the Bible—is that science *hasn't*, in fact, explained the miracles recorded in the Bible. And it *can't*. So why on earth should we believe the much *larger* claim that science has somehow *proved* that such things can't ever happen at all, no way, no how?

The answer is that we shouldn't. To put it bluntly, this objection outruns its own jogging shorts. It's just not the case that science has *proven* that the supernatural does not and cannot happen. Plenty of things happen in the universe—and in human experience—that science cannot explain. Don't misunderstand me. I'm not saying that anything science can't explain must be supernatural. No, science will advance, and it will answer many questions in the future that it cannot answer now. But no scientist truly in tune with the promise *and the limits* of science—especially with the latest advances in fields like quantum physics, astronomy, even biology—would ever say anything like, "The universe is and evermore shall be utterly explicable." In fact, such a scientist would probably say something more like, "You know, the more we discover, the more we realize how much we really do not understand and indeed how much may be finally beyond understanding."

Besides, the whole question of whether miracles are possible ultimately comes down to whether there is a God, right? If there is, then miracles are possible, full stop. But everyone agrees that science completely lacks the ability to test whether God exists. It will never *prove* that there's no God, and therefore it will never prove that miracles are impossible. In that light, the flippant, smug declaration I've heard so many fresh-man science majors make that "science has proven that super-natural things absolutely, positively cannot happen" begins to sound just embarrassingly flimsy.

## Arguments against Miracles— The Philosophical Objection

A second objection lodged against the plausibility of miracles is a *philosophical* one. It says that, even if science can't prove the *impossibility* of miracles (a significant concession, let's no-tice!), we should still say that the *probability* of a miraculous event actually happening is vanishingly small, and therefore we should never believe it. For example, we should never believe that Jesus actually walked on water because if $X$ stands for ev-eryone who's ever tried to walk on water and sunk (to be safe, let's just put that number at ten billion, a rough estimate of everyone who's ever lived on the planet), then the probability of Jesus having actually walked on water is about one in ten billion. Not very high.

But come on. This objection ends up proving way too much. You can't just run probabilities on everything like that to determine if you're going to believe it or not. If you did, you'd have to doubt *everything* that's unusual or uncommon, much less unique. There are about seven billion people in the world today, but as far as we know, only *one* has run the 100-meter dash in 9.58 seconds. Even so, it would be absurd and arrogant of me to say, "Humph. Do you realize the probability of Usain Bolt having run the 100-meter in 9.58 seconds is one in seven billion? It would be stupid for me to believe it." In the same way, just because it's astonishing to think of Jesus walking on water doesn't mean it didn't happen. After all, the disciples themselves were pretty astonished at it too, which was precisely why they wrote it down.

So there we are. Naturally, skeptics formulate lots of different variations on these two arguments, but none of them ultimately ends up doing any better than these two at excluding miracles or the supernatural from the realm of human reality. Science hasn't offered an explanation of the things the biblical writers tell us they saw, and it *certainly* hasn't proven that such things are impossible. Moreover, it simply doesn't make any sense to decide what's plausible based on probabilities. The fact is, if you're going to assert that the supernatural doesn't happen (ever, at all), you're going to have to do just that—*assert it*, without evidence, for really no good reason. In other words, you're going to have to believe it on the worst kind of blind faith.

## Are the Biblical Miracles Plausible?

So the biblical writers said they saw extraordinary things happen, and we have no logical reason to say that those things are inherently impossible or even hopelessly implausible. But there's still one other question that comes up here. Lots of people have told lots of stories about "miraculous" things happening. The Babylonians did. The Greeks did. So did the Romans. And nobody says we ought to believe *their* miracle stories. So why is the Bible any different? What makes its stories any more plausible than theirs? Well, the answer is that the character of the biblical writings just utterly differs from the character of those other ancient writings *in ways that make them eminently more plausible.*

Let me explain what I mean. In other ancient miracle stories, we're obviously not dealing with eyewitness accounts of historical events; they don't even claim to be that. Rather, we're quite clearly dealing with either (1) legends or myths that have arisen and been repeatedly augmented—like barnacles growing on a ship—over the course of several centuries, or (2) originally unremarkable historical stories that were subsequently embellished with supernatural bits that, while truly amazing, are still more or less gratuitous. By that I mean that the supernatural events in those stories don't seem in any way *essential* to the story itself; the story would make perfect sense without the supernatural parts, which suggests that those bits were added later for effect. The point is that in both cases, historians can look at those ancient stories and conclude very confidently that the miraculous details are not historical. They're either myths and legends that have been built up over time, or they're superfluous embellishments added for effect. But they are decidedly not eyewitness accounts of events without which the entire story makes no sense.

That, however, is *precisely* the character of the miracle accounts in the Bible. They are neither myths nor legends. They have not been built up over centuries. They are the result of some person saying, "I saw this, and I saw it not so very long ago." Not only that but the miracles recorded in the Bible are essential to the stories around them. Jesus's miracles, for instance, are not just amazing things that happened. When you study them, you realize that right down to their very core, they're connected to the message Jesus was proclaiming. That's why Jesus heals people rather than just pulling a rabbit out of a hat; he's illustrating that he can heal people from the disease of sin. It's why he raises people from the dead instead of making a coin disappear down his sleeve; he's showing how his work brings spiritual life out of spiritual death. Even his walking on the water wasn't just a parlor trick; his disciples recognized that it confirmed his claim to be the great "I am," the One who brings the ocean—the ancient realm of chaos and evil—into submission, the One who, as the psalm puts it, is "mightier than the waves of the sea" (Ps. 93:4). The miracle stories of other religions and cultures are nothing like that.

Do you see the point? The miracles of the Bible are not in any way superfluous or extraneous to the stories in which we find them; on the contrary, they are essential to them, woven like DNA into their very meaning. Moreover, rather than legends or myths built up over time, they are eyewitness accounts of what real people said they saw with their own eyes. However you slice it, the biblical miracle accounts differ utterly from a Greek or Babylonian myth, and they require a whole different kind of reckoning.

All this leaves us with a pretty significant conclusion about the miracles recorded in the Bible: they cannot be kicked out of court as being logically impossible, and they are far more plausible than other "miracle" stories out there. Still, I wonder if we can go even farther. Can we get to a level of confidence that would allow us to say not just that it's *plausible* that what the biblical authors are saying actually happened but that it's actually historically *probable* that they did?

I think we can.

## Everything Rests on the Resurrection

Now at this point, we have a couple choices about how we could proceed. We could begin an exhaustive study of the dozens of miracles that Jesus did throughout his ministry and see what we can say about each of them. Many books, in fact, have done just that, and their conclusions are often insightful and convincing (see appendix). Or we could go straight to the one miracle that underlies and indeed launched the entire Christian faith, the one on which the whole superstructure of Christian history, belief, and practice ultimately rests—indeed, the one on which the Christian belief that the Bible is the Word of God finally rests.

That's the resurrection of Jesus.

Here's what you really can't get around: If the resurrection happened, then the rest of the fundamental superstructure of Christianity comes together like clockwork—including the authority of the Bible, both New Testament and Old. If it *didn't* happen, then never mind any of it, because if our reliable biblical writers turn out to have been wrong about the resurrection—the most important thing—then it's unlikely that they were right about much of anything. And besides, it wouldn't matter whether or not they were right about the rest, because the very point of *everything*—the miracles, the teaching, the claims—was to demonstrate the identity of Jesus as the Christ, and if he's still dead, then he's not the Christ, and therefore the rest of it doesn't matter, full stop. The whole of Christianity rises or falls on the question of whether Jesus historically—not religiously or spiritually but *historically*—was resurrected from the dead.

The biblical writers thought he was. They weren't deluded, they weren't trying to pull off a hoax, and they weren't writing a legend. They were telling it like they saw it, heard it, touched it, and experienced it, and they genuinely wanted their readers to believe it too. All well and good. But can we have any confidence that they were right about it?

Yes, we can. But how?

## Why They Believed Jesus Was Resurrected

Let's start by asking the obvious question. In their own telling, what made the biblical writers—and the early Christians more broadly—believe that Jesus had been resurrected in the first place? According to their own testimony, that belief really emerged from two things: (1) their discovery on Sunday morning that the tomb where Jesus's body had been laid after his death was empty, and (2) their experience of Jesus appearing to them after his death multiple times in physical form.

Now it's important to realize a few things about these experiences. For one, the authors are dead set on denying that what they saw when Jesus appeared to them was something incorporeal (that is, without a physical body), like a ghost or a spirit or something. So Luke is careful to point out that the first time Jesus appeared to the disciples, they actually thought he was a ghost until Jesus invited them to touch him—"a spirit does not have flesh and bones as you see that I have," he said— and then ate a piece of broiled fish just to prove the point (Luke 24:39, 42–43). (It's interesting that the account mentions that the fish was broiled, isn't it? What does the fact that the fish was broiled, rather than baked or grilled or sautéed, have to do with anything? Nothing. It's just one of those details that a legend probably wouldn't include and that therefore subtly suggests that this is real eyewitness testimony from someone who was there.)

Not only that, but the disciples are also at pains to make the point that this person who appeared to them *was the same Jesus who died on the cross*, not someone else. "Put your finger here, and see my hands; and put out your hand, and place it in my side," Jesus told Thomas (John 20:27). He wasn't a ghost; he wasn't somebody else. The apostles insisted that the Jesus they saw was the same Jesus who had been crucified.

It's also important to understand that neither the empty tomb nor the appearances alone would have created the kind of certainty about the resurrection that the apostles ultimately displayed. If all they had was the empty tomb, they would have gone away scratching their heads for sure, but it's doubtful they would have concluded that Jesus had come back to life. Too many alternatives could have explained it: grave robbers, some further humiliation by the Romans, a mistake in locating the tomb, something!

At the same time, simply seeing Jesus wouldn't have done it either. Again, there were just too many other explanations:

a ghost, an apparition, an impostor, anything! So long as a decomposing corpse could be produced from the tomb, certainly no one could call this whole thing a resurrection.

But put the two together—an empty tomb and the appearances of Jesus—and it was enough to create a nuclear explosion in the disciples' reality. The tomb was empty because Jesus was alive. "He is not here," the angel said, "for he has risen" (Matt. 28:6). That's their testimony. That's the reason they believed, and that's the reason they ultimately died for the belief that Jesus really did rise from the grave. Now you can say you don't believe them; you can say that whatever happened on that Sunday morning, it wasn't *that*. But if you're going to do that, then you have to offer some alternative. If not the resurrection, then what *did* happen?

## Nothing Else Explains It

Look, the one thing you can't do (not with any intellectual honesty, anyway) is pretend that *nothing* happened. Clearly something *did*, because it has created shockwaves around the world and throughout history for two thousand years. Even just in the lives of those disciples, whatever it was that happened caused them to rearrange the very structure of their worldview. They began to believe that this crucified Jesus was the long-awaited Messiah of Jewish hope, that he was the Son of God, the vindicated, sin-bearing Lamb of God, the first-fruits of a new creation that would begin in his own redeemed people, the King of kings who would one day save his people finally and forever and remake the world in a new birth reflective of and flowing from his own resurrection life. Because they believed these things, they rearranged their lives so that they could proclaim their beliefs—abandoning careers, leaving homes, and ultimately refusing to back away from those beliefs even as (according to tradition) they were, one by one, beheaded, crucified, impaled with spears, flayed, and stoned.

*Something* happened to cause all that.

And either it was that Jesus really was resurrected from the dead, or it was something else that would have been powerful enough to cause the disciples—all at once—to embrace those beliefs and rearrange their lives to proclaim them, even in the face of gruesome martyrdoms. So that's really the last question: Has anyone ever suggested any other alternative that has the power to explain all that? Certainly, a lot of people have made a lot of attempts.

Maybe the women went to the wrong tomb and just got everyone excited over a mistake. Perhaps. But then, when a belief that this Jesus had been resurrected was spreading through the city like wildfire, why didn't the authorities just produce a corpse from the *right* tomb? Surely they knew where it was, given that the Roman guard placed a seal on it. And besides, as we've already said, the mere report that the tomb was empty wouldn't have created a belief that Jesus had been resurrected. Jesus also *appeared* to the disciples, alive! That's what they (reliably) told us. If you're going to say they were wrong, fine. But what—if not that—did happen?

Okay, maybe Jesus didn't really die but only *almost* died, eventually escaped from the tomb, and made his way back to where his disciples were hiding. Perhaps. But then why . . . actually, no, not perhaps. That's absurd! Are we really to think that Jesus—somehow managing to survive his crucifixion— staggered wounded, crucified, spear-stabbed, and now de- hydrated and starving into the presence of his disciples and convinced them, frightened and skeptical though they were, that he was the Lord of life and the Conqueror of death? Not highly likely, I'd say. They wouldn't have gone out to preach at that point; they would have gotten him a doctor!

Alright, well, maybe the disciples stole the body and then claimed that Jesus was raised from the dead; maybe it was the most successful hoax in the history of the world. But no, like we said before, nothing about this has the character of a hoax, and above all, nobody dies for a hoax. If you're just trying to pull one over on the world, when the jig is up and the axe is about to fall—or the nails are about to pierce your wrists, or they're about to drop you in the boiling oil or throw you off the top of the temple—you don't keep on saying, "I tell you, the man is alive!" The only way you stick by the story under those circumstances *is if you really believe it's true.*

Well, maybe the disciples were the victims of mass hallu- cination. No, we've already discussed that suggestion at some length. Given how many different groups of people reported seeing Jesus, how many different times, and over how many weeks, the notion of a sustained, contagious mass hallucina- tion is vanishingly unlikely. And of course, the idea of a "mass hallucination" is absurd in itself.

Perhaps, then, they were overwhelmed by a dream, a vision, a mystical experience, or even a profound and heavenly feeling of forgiveness and new spiritual life. Maybe that's what they meant by using the term *resurrection* and not this grossly literal idea that Jesus actually got up from the grave. In other words, maybe all the stories in the New Testament are just one big metaphor for spiritual truths, not meant to be taken literally and physically.

No, the fact is, first of all, that the accounts of the resurrection simply don't have the character of spiritual metaphors. They have the character of eyewitness testimony to events that physically happened in history, and it would take a great deal of blurring the eyes to get past that. Also, the first-century Jewish world was not unfamiliar with dreams or visions or ecstatic religious experiences, nor was it unfamiliar with would-be messiahs whom the authorities killed off. Given that background, it's just unthinkable that a mere dream, vision, or mystical experience, much less a feeling—even if it was connected to an executed "messiah"—could have given rise to the kind of enduring, worldview-altering belief in Jesus's resurrection that marked the first Christians and drove their martyr's resolve. Most of all, though, no first-century Jew would ever have used the word *resurrection* to describe a dream, vision, or mystical experience, much less a "feeling" of whatever kind or strength. That's because *resurrection* had a very specific meaning. It meant the literal, physical coming-back-to-life of the body, and it would emphatically *not* be used to refer to anything short of that. Yet that's *exactly* the word the early Christians used to describe what happened to Jesus.

Okay, so maybe they were all victims of a severe case of wishful thinking. Maybe they just wanted *so badly* for Jesus not to have died that they fooled themselves into believing he had been resurrected. Again, no. Even if the disciples were searching for comfort in the wake of Jesus's death, they wouldn't have reached for the idea of resurrection. It's far more likely that they would have comforted themselves by claiming he was "spiritually" alive or something. But it's just implausible in the extreme to think that they would have lit upon the worldview-reshaping idea that Jesus had been resurrected and glorified before the end of time. The only way they would have arrived at that conclusion is if the things they had seen and experienced *left them with no other choice.* Do you see the point? The early Christians didn't claim that Jesus had been resurrected because of a *wish.* They made that claim because there was no other explanation for what they saw. It wasn't wishful thinking that led them to that conclusion; it was their own eyes.

On top of that, the accounts we have just don't present the disciples as in any way intellectually prepared to believe that Jesus had risen from the dead. To the contrary, long before they believed, they *dis*believed in a big way, to the point that the resurrected Jesus had to rebuke them for it. No, the disciples were not in *any way* psychologically, religiously, or culturally prepared for the resurrection of one man before the end of time. That such a thing might actually have happened quite truly exploded into their consciousness and left them struggling to explain what it all meant.

So like I said, something happened that Sunday morning. There's simply no denying that.

And now I'm asking you, *what was it*? It was not a mistake, not a near death, not a hoax or deception, not a mass hallucination, not a dream or vision or mystical feeling of forgiveness, not wishful thinking—none of these things. So if not these, then *what was it*?

Look, when you come right down to it, the evidence before us—the early Christians' confident insistence that the tomb was empty and that they saw the risen Jesus, the life-altering beliefs that flowed from those experiences, their resolute embracing of their faith even in the face of death—this evidence is explained by only one possibility:

> Jesus was really, truly, bodily, historically *resurrected from the dead*.

## Implications of a Resurrected Jesus

It's hardly worth saying it, but all this isn't something we can simply rush past, is it? It's all of enormous, even eternal, importance. So as we close this chapter, let me cede the page to one particularly well-known scholar, N. T. Wright, who puts the conclusion of the matter very helpfully. Read it slowly, read it carefully, and think it all through one more time:

> [That Jesus was resurrected] remains, of course, unprovable in logical or mathematical terms. The historian is never in a position to do what Pythagoras did. . . . With history it is not like that. Almost nothing is ever ruled out absolutely;

history, after all, is mostly the study of the unusual and unre-
peatable. What we are after is high probability; and this is to
be attained by examining all the possibilities, all the sugges-
tions, and asking how well they explain the phenomena. It is
always possible that in discussing the resurrection someone
will come up with the skeptical critic's dream: an explanation which provides a sufficient condition for the rise of early
Christian faith but which, by fitting into post-Enlightenment
epistemological and ontological categories, or even simply
mainstream pagan ones, causes no fluttering in the critical
dovecotes. It is worthy of note that, despite the somewhat
desperate attempts of many scholars over the last two hundred years (not to mention critics since at least Celsus), no
such explanation has been found. The early Christians did
not invent the empty tomb and the "meetings" or "sightings"
of the risen Jesus in order to explain a faith they already
had. They developed that faith because of the occurrence,
and convergence, of these two phenomena. Nobody was ex-
pecting this kind of thing; no kind of conversion-experience
would have generated such ideas; nobody would have in-
vented it, no matter how guilty (or how forgiven) they felt, no
matter how many hours they pored over the scriptures. To
suggest otherwise is to stop doing history and to enter into
a fantasy world of our own, a new cognitive dissonance in
which the relentless modernist, desperately worried that the
post-Enlightenment worldview seems in imminent danger of
collapse, devises strategies for shoring it up nevertheless. In
terms of the kind of proof which historians normally accept,
the case we have presented, that the tomb-plus-appearances

combination is what generated early Christian belief, is as watertight as one is likely to find.[3]

We've come a long way in our consideration of whether we really can trust the Bible, haven't we? Despite the fact that we face questions at every turn, we've been able to come to a high degree of historical confidence that the Bible really is reliable. Here's what we've seen: Our translations are correct; the copies we have are faithful reproductions of the originals (or, at the very least, they allow us to reconstruct the originals); the documents we're looking at are the best and correct ones; the authors themselves weren't dupes or deceitful or writers of fiction (they were telling us what they really believed happened); and finally, we have very good reason to believe that what they *thought* happened and what they *said* happened really did in fact happen. The miracles they recount can't be ruled out in principle, and their plausibility far surpasses any other historical accounts of supernatural happenings. Above all, when it comes to the most important miracle of all—the resurrection of Jesus—no explanation really makes sense of all the evidence other than that *it happened*.

But here's the last step in our argument. If the resurrection happened, then our trust of the Bible is actually catapulted to a whole new level of confidence, far beyond the mere historical kind.

If Jesus was really resurrected from the dead, then the Bible is the Word of God.

---

[3] Wright, *The Resurrection of the Son of God*, 706–7.

# 7

# Take It on the Word of a Resurrected Man

In some ways, I really wish this book could have ended with the previous chapter.

I wish the weight of the whole thing could rest on what we just discussed, because I believe that's the most important truth claim in human history: that we can best explain the evidence before us if Jesus really did rise bodily from the grave. So even though I hope you'll read the rest of the book, I also hope you'll be most captured and most fascinated by thinking about that conclusion and its implications. What does it mean for you if Jesus was, in fact, resurrected? What would you need to *do* to respond to that reality?

But since this book is titled *Why Trust the Bible?* and not *Why Trust That Jesus Rose from the Dead?*, we should press that question to its conclusion. Throughout this book, we have been thinking and talking about the biblical documents—especially the New Testament and even more so the four Gospels—as *historical documents*. In doing so, we have not presupposed that they are divine or from God in any way. We haven't presupposed that they are the Word of God, and we haven't presupposed that they're without error or always true. In fact, just as we would do for any other document we might find buried in the ruins of an ancient village, we have allowed for every possibility that the biblical documents might be unreliable as historical witnesses. But at every turn, we've also concluded with a high degree of historical confidence that they *do* in fact seem reliable—from our *translations*, to the *transmission* of the original documents through history by copyists, to the reception of *these* documents as opposed to any others as authoritative, to the *trustworthiness* of the authors themselves, to the very *truth* of what they wrote about. From start to finish, we've created a strong chain of confidence that the Bible is reliable as a witness to history.

But when we as Christians say we trust the Bible, we don't mean that we have a strong *historical confidence* in it. We mean much more than that. We mean that we believe it is the Word of God, inspired by the Creator of the universe so that it is absolutely, unfailingly true in everything it says. Here, for example, is how my church's "Statement of Faith" puts it:

> We believe that the Bible, specifically the 39 books of the Old Testament and the 27 books of the New Testament, is the written Word of God; that it was written by men divinely inspired, and is a perfect treasure of heavenly instruction; that it has God for its author, salvation for its end, and truth without any mixture of error for its matter; that it reveals the principles by which God will judge us; and therefore is, and shall remain to the end

of the world, the true center of Christian union, and the only sufficient, certain and authoritative rule of all saving knowledge, faith, and obedience.[1]

Everyone who is a member of our church believes that the Bible—New Testament *and* Old—is "the written Word of God," that it was written by men who were "divinely inspired," that it is a "perfect treasure of heavenly instruction," that it "has God for its author," and even that it is by nature "truth without any mixture of error." Obviously, that all goes way past historical confidence!

We don't have time or space here to think carefully about everything Christians mean when they say these things. Topics like *inspiration* and *inerrancy* have demanded books all their own (see appendix). What's important for our purposes is that we understand why Christians say all these exalted things about the Bible in the first place. And to put it simply, it's because Jesus rose from the dead. Because of Jesus's resurrection, we believe what Jesus said, and since Jesus himself endorsed the entire Old Testament and authorized the entire New, we believe they are reliable and true. That's pretty much it.

## The Messiah *Will* Rise from the Dead

To Christians, the resurrection means many important things. It means that those of us who are united to Jesus by faith will be resurrected just like he was. It means that God fully accepted

[1] "What We Believe," Third Avenue Baptist Church, Louisville, KY, accessed February 25, 2015, http://www.thirdavenue.org/What-We-Believe.

the sacrifice for sins that Jesus offered on the cross and that it was infinitely more than sufficient to pay our moral debt. It means that Jesus now lives to lead, rule, protect, intercede for, and do good for his people who are still alive on earth. And it also means that God ratified, endorsed, vindicated, and confirmed all of Jesus's claims about who he was and what kind of authority he possessed.

That's not a difficult point to grasp. Like all the other miracles, Jesus's resurrection was no superfluous addition to the story, just a flourish needed to ensure a good ending. When Jesus talked about it, he always tightly connected it to his claims about his identity. Matthew, for instance, tells us that Jesus predicted his death and resurrection three times near the end of his ministry, and each time, he presented it as *the necessary and confirming culmination of his identity as the Christ.* Let's look at those three predictions.

First, Jesus once asked his disciples who they thought he was, and Peter responded, "You are the Christ, the Son of the living God" (Matt. 16:16). Now that phrase holds a world of meaning, but essentially Peter was affirming that Jesus was the long-promised, long-prophesied, long-awaited Messiah (meaning "anointed one" and therefore King) of Israel and that he was also the Son of God (which is to say that he *was* God). Hearing this, Jesus rejoiced and told Peter that he was blessed to have had this knowledge revealed to him by God the Father. Then Jesus began to act as the King that Peter had just acknowledged him to be. He established his church—his royal embassy in the world—and promised that he would protect it and empower it in its mission. He gave that embassy authority to speak in his name, and then, crucially, he began to teach the disciples what it actually meant that he was in fact the King, the Messiah, the Christ. So Matthew (remember, he was there!) tells us the following:

> From that time Jesus began to show his disciples that he must go to Jerusalem and suffer many things from the elders and chief priests and scribes, and be killed, and on the third day be raised. (Matt. 16:21)

Notice first the way Matthew puts this: "From that time Jesus began to show his disciples." Apparently this was not a one-time, five-minute conversation, but a staple of Jesus's teaching from that point on. Also, notice the word "must." He "must" go to Jerusalem and suffer and be killed, and he "must" be raised from the dead on the third day. Now notice the word "show." What does it mean that he began to "show" them that all this must happen? Show them from what? Logic? Reason? No, it means that he showed them from the Scriptures, from the Old Testament. Okay, do you see the point? The role, the mission, and therefore the destiny of the Messiah was not something "to be determined"; it was all well defined in the Old Testament, Jesus explained, and one of the things the true Messiah *would do* is be resurrected. "The Messiah will rise from the dead," Jesus was saying. "So if I don't rise from the dead, then I'm not the Messiah. But *I will*. And therefore . . ."—you get the point.

Jesus predicted his death a second time a few days later, and this time he connected it with another Old Testament prophecy of the Messiah. Here's how Matthew tells it:

> As they were gathering in Galilee, Jesus said to them, "The Son of Man is about to be delivered into the hands of men, and they will kill him, and he will be raised on the third day." And they were greatly distressed. (Matt. 17:22)

*Son of Man* was apparently Jesus's favorite way to talk about his identity, but it doesn't just mean "a man's son." That would describe quite a lot of us. Rather, he took the title from the Old Testament prophet Daniel, who had a vision of what he called "one like a son of man." Now that means, simply, that the one Daniel saw looked like a human. But notice what Daniel says that "one like a son of man" did:

> I saw in the night visions,
>> and behold, with the clouds of heaven
>>> there came one like a son of man,
>> and he came to the Ancient of Days
>>> and was presented before him.
>> And to him was given dominion
>>> and glory and a kingdom,
>> that all peoples, nations, and languages
>>> should serve him;
>> his dominion is an everlasting dominion,
>>> which shall not pass away,
>> and his kingdom one
>>> that shall not be destroyed. (Dan. 7:13–14)

That's what Jesus was referring to when he called himself *Son of Man*. This massively significant title pointed not only to royal authority but to divinity itself. Most important for our purposes, though, notice again how Jesus connected all these allusions specifically to the resurrection in Matthew 17:22 above. No, he doesn't use the word *must* here, but the effect is the same. He means, "*Just like the Old Testament prophesied,* the Son of Man is about to be killed and raised again on the third day. If that doesn't happen, then I'm not the Son of Man. But I *am* the Son of Man, so all this is about to take place."

The third time Jesus predicted his resurrection in Matthew's Gospel was right before he went into Jerusalem just days prior to his crucifixion. Here's how Matthew records what he said:

> And as Jesus was going up to Jerusalem, he took the twelve disciples aside, and on the way he said to them, "See, we are going up to Jerusalem. And the Son of Man will be delivered over to the chief priests and scribes, and they will condemn him to death and deliver him over to the Gentiles to be mocked and flogged and crucified, and he will be raised on the third day. (Matt. 20:17–19)

There's really not much new here. Jesus makes the same point that he made in the previous prediction: "Because I'm the Son of Man, this *is* about to happen."

Do you see? Jesus always connected his resurrection with his identity. If it happened, then he was the Messiah, the Christ, the King, the Son of Man. If not—well, then, never mind. After the resurrection, the apostles did the same thing. Peter's sermon in Acts 2 is crystal clear in this regard. Here's what he said:

> Men of Israel, hear these words: Jesus of Nazareth, a man attested to you by God with mighty works and wonders and signs that God did through him in your midst, as you yourselves know—this Jesus, delivered up according to the definite plan and foreknowledge of God, you crucified and killed by the hands of lawless men. God raised him up, loosing the pangs of death, because it was not possible for him to be held by it. For David says concerning him,
>
>> "I saw the Lord always before me,
>>> for he is at my right hand that I may not be shaken;
>> therefore my heart was glad, and my tongue rejoiced;
>>> my flesh also will dwell in hope.
>> For you will not abandon my soul to Hades,
>>> or let your Holy One see corruption.
>> You have made known to me the paths of life;
>>> you will make me full of gladness with your presence."
>
> Brothers, I may say to you with confidence about the patriarch David that he both died and was buried, and his tomb is with us to this day. Being therefore a prophet, and knowing that God had sworn with an oath to him that he would set one of his descendants on his throne, he

foresaw and spoke about the resurrection of the Christ, that he was not abandoned to Hades, nor did his flesh see corruption. This Jesus God raised up, and of that we all are witnesses. Being therefore exalted at the right hand of God, and having received from the Father the promise of the Holy Spirit, he has poured out this that you yourselves are seeing and hearing. For David did not ascend into the heavens, but he himself says,

> "The Lord said to my Lord,
> 'Sit at my right hand,
>     until I make your enemies your footstool.'"

Let all the house of Israel therefore know for certain that God has made him both Lord and Christ, this Jesus whom you crucified. (Acts 2:22–36)

Do you see what he's saying? Here's the gist: "You guys put Jesus to death, but God raised him to life again because it was impossible for death to hold him. Why? Because as David said, God would not let the Messiah see the decay of death. Now David *couldn't* have been talking about himself being the Messiah, because he died and was buried and we know where his tomb is to this day. So he must have been talking about a future Messiah. Well, guess what? God raised up this Jesus—we are all eyewitnesses of that fact. Therefore, because the Messiah would be raised, and because Jesus was raised, *let all the house of Israel know for certain that God has made this Jesus—whom you crucified—both Lord and Christ.*"

Peter couldn't be any clearer. Jesus had been resurrected, and therefore Jesus was the Christ, just as he said.

## What Does the Resurrection Mean for the Old Testament?

What, though, do Jesus's resurrection and self-identification as the Christ have to do with the Bible? Everything. The Old Testament taught that the authority of the Messiah would be all-encompassing, multifaceted, universal, and absolute. He would hold sway in every area of life and existence. But one particular area in which he would have authority was in *speaking for God the Father*. In other words, he would be a prophet par excellence. God even said that he would send a prophet like Moses and promised, "I will put my words in his mouth, and he shall speak to them all that I command him" (Deut. 18:18). That's why Jesus could say something as audacious as, "Truly, truly, I say to you, the Son can do nothing of his own accord, but only what he sees the Father doing. For whatever the Father does, that the Son does likewise" (John 5:19). And it's why John would say of Jesus, "For he whom God has sent utters the words of God" (John 3:34). The Christ was also *the* Prophet, the One who reveals perfectly who God is and what God says.

Understanding that, it's remarkable to see how Jesus—the Christ, the Prophet, the One who would hold perfect authority to speak for God—treated the Old Testament throughout his ministry. Take, for instance, Luke's account of what Jesus said to his disciples after his resurrection:

Then he said to them, "These are my words that I spoke to you while I was still with you, that everything written about me in the Law of Moses and the Prophets and the Psalms must be fulfilled." (Luke 24:44)

Now the Jews often used a shorthand to refer to the books of their Old Testament, either "the Law, the Prophets, and the Writings" or, more simply, "the Law and the Prophets." So when Jesus said that "the Law of Moses and the Prophets and the Psalms" (the book of Psalms representing the Writings as the largest book in that collection) must be fulfilled, he was endorsing and ratifying the authority of the entire Old Testament from start to finish. (Incidentally, he was also clearly defining the scope of the Old Testament canon to be the thirty-nine books traditionally recognized by the Jews.)

But Jesus's testimony about the Old Testament runs even deeper. He not only thought it was authoritative; he said it was the very Word of God. Look at this passage from Matthew 19:

And Pharisees came up to him and tested him by asking, "Is it lawful to divorce one's wife for any cause?" He answered, "Have you not read that he who created them from the beginning made them male and female, and said, 'Therefore a man shall leave his father and his mother and hold fast to his wife, and the two shall become one flesh'? So they are no longer two but one flesh. What therefore God has joined together, let not man separate." (vv. 3–6)

The story here is that some of Israel's leaders were questioning Jesus about his understanding of Scripture. Clearly, they were less interested in what he had to say than in trapping and discrediting him. How the exchange went down is fascinating in itself, but what I want you to see is that Jesus identified the One who said, "Therefore a man shall leave his father and his mother," as "he who created them [husband and wife]." The interesting thing, though, is that if you take a look back at Genesis, you'll notice that this sentence is not attributed to God at all. Rather, it's a commentary on the situation by the *human author* of Genesis. But therein lies the point: Jesus understood even the parts of the Old Testament where God wasn't actually speaking *as the words of God*.

You can see the same thing in Mark 12:36 where Jesus quotes a psalm written by David, but introduces it by saying, "David himself, in the Holy Spirit, declared . . ." You see? From start to finish, Jesus the Messiah endorsed and confirmed that every word of the Old Testament was the Word of God and therefore true from start to finish. That was the case for its teaching about God, and according to Jesus, it was also the case for its historical claims. At some point in the four Gospels, Jesus talks about and treats as historically accurate all kinds of people and stories from the Old Testament—Adam and Eve, Cain and Abel, Noah, Abraham, Sodom and Gomorrah, Isaac, Jacob, Moses, the manna falling in the wilderness, the bronze serpent, David and Solomon, the Queen of Sheba, Elijah and Elisha, the widow of Zarephath, Naaman, Isaiah, Jeremiah, Zechariah, and even Jonah getting swallowed by the giant fish.

He believed it all in every detail. And that matters because he was the Christ.

Now sometimes people will trip at this point and say, "But didn't Jesus actually *correct* some places of the Old Testament? Didn't he think some places of it were wrong or inadequate and tell his followers to believe something different?" Well, no. There were certainly times when Jesus said things like, "You have heard that it was said . . . but I say to you . . ." We don't have time to consider these occasions in detail (you can find thorough explanations in any good Bible commentary), but the thing to realize is that at each of these points, Jesus wasn't correcting the Old Testament. He was correcting wrong, disingenuous, and even malicious attempts by the Pharisees to dodge the true meaning of the Old Testament or carve out ridiculous exceptions for themselves. That means that far from *correcting* the Old Testament, Jesus was actually exercising his kingly, prophetic authority to *say what the Old Testament really meant in the first place*—that is, to reassert its power, authority, and truth in the lives of the Israelites. Thus he explained before he began to do just that in his famous Sermon on the Mount, "Do not think that I have come to abolish the Law or the Prophets; I have not come to abolish them but to fulfill them" (Matt. 5:17).

Do you see the point? Of course there are still going to be questions about hermeneutics and interpretation, how we should understand this and how that fits into the Christian life, covenants and dispensations and all the rest. Moreover, the Old Testament presents its own unique issues regarding transmission, canonization, and authorship, and you can read large books by Christian scholars about all these topics (see appendix). But here's the important thing. Here's why *all* those large books will begin with the belief that the Old Testament is the Word of God: because Jesus, the resurrected Messiah, said it was. And therefore we believe it.

## What Does the Resurrection Mean for the New Testament?

So now what about the New Testament? Frankly, things are not quite as straightforward when it comes to the New Testament. After all, when Jesus was on earth and could have verbally confirmed the authority of the New Testament as he did with the Old, the New Testament hadn't yet been written.

Even so, Christians' belief that the New Testament is the Word of God also goes back to the authority of Jesus as the resurrected Messiah, just in a slightly different way. Do you remember how, in chapter 4 of this book, we said that the early Christians always talked about authoritative, canonical books being *handed down* to them and that the main and primary criterion they used to defend those books was that they had apostolic authority? At that point, we simply noted the reasonability of that assertion as a historical matter; of course it makes sense to have the most confidence in books that came with a stamp of approval from eyewitnesses.

But that's not the only—or even primary—reason that apostolicity was the early church's main criterion for confirming the exclusive authority of those received books. The primary reason goes back, again, to the authority of Jesus. You see, in John 16, when Jesus was giving final instructions to his apostles, he promised that after his resurrection and ascension into heaven, he would send the Holy Spirit to relay to them further teaching that he wanted them to have. It's really an extraordinary passage:

> [Jesus said,] "I still have many things to say to you, but you cannot bear them now. When the Spirit of truth comes, he will guide you into all the truth, for he will not speak on his own authority, but whatever he hears he will speak, and he will declare to you the things that are to come. He will glorify me, for he will take what is mine and declare it to you. All that the Father has is mine; therefore I said that he will take what is mine and declare it to you." (vv. 12–15)

That's an amazing chain of authority Jesus constructs, isn't it? Everything he has to say is from the Father (there's that prophetic authority again), and he will give all that comes from the Father to the Holy Spirit, who will in turn declare it to the apostles. Do you see? Jesus is here telling his apostles that more teaching will come and that it will come to *them* in particular. It's interesting to see how the apostles themselves, in their writings, seem to have realized that they were writing with that kind of Spirit-inspired, Scripture-making authority. One passage is especially important. In 2 Peter 3, the apostle Peter is encouraging his readers to stand firm until the end. Then he says:

> And count the patience of our Lord as salvation, just as
> our beloved brother Paul also wrote to you according to
> the wisdom given him, as he does in all his letters when
> he speaks in them of these matters. There are some things
> in them that are hard to understand, which the ignorant
> and unstable twist to their own destruction, as they do the
> other Scriptures. (vv. 15–16)

It's amusing to note that Peter thought Paul's writings were
"hard to understand." Not a few other Christians have had the
same feeling themselves sometimes! But Peter also says that
Paul wrote "according to the wisdom given to him, as he does
in all his letters." That's not just regular wisdom he's talking
about; it's a throwback to Jesus's promise to the apostles that
he would send the Holy Spirit to lead them into all truth. Then
at the end, Peter says that "ignorant and unstable" people will
sometimes twist Paul's words to their own ends *just like they
do the other Scriptures*! Clearly, Peter was putting Paul's writings on the same rarefied level of authority as the Old Testament Scriptures. They were a fulfillment of exactly what Jesus
had promised to do through the Holy Spirit.

This chain of authority explains why the early Christians
emphasized so strongly the need to trace a canonical document
back to the apostles. It wasn't *just* that those men were eyewitnesses; it was that they had been *particularly and specifically
authorized* by the King to teach the church the rest of what he
wanted taught.

Now in chapter 4 we concluded that we can have a great
deal of confidence that the books of our New Testament are

in fact the books that carry this kind of authority. If you need to go back and read that chapter again, do it. There's plenty of *historical* evidence that we do in fact have the right books. But it's worth pointing out that, *as Christians*, our confidence that the New Testament represents precisely what Jesus *meant* for us to have isn't based merely on historical evidence; it's based on the understanding that part of the Holy Spirit's job of "guid[ing] you into all the truth" (John 16:13), would have included guiding the process of canonization too. I mean, once you come to the conclusion that Jesus was resurrected from death and therefore that he's the King of the universe, it's a really short hop to the conclusion that he's well and truly capable of making sure the "all truth" he promised was pulled together correctly.

So there you have it. If Jesus was resurrected, then he is the long-awaited Messiah, Christ, King, Son of God, and Prophet par excellence. And if that's true, then we'd better pay attention to him, including his endorsement of the entire Old Testament as the Word of God. Not only that, but we have every reason to trust that he did precisely what he promised he would do—send the Holy Spirit to guide his apostles into all the truth he wanted to reveal to them for the good of the church—and then to trust the Spirit's work of guiding the church in recognizing that truth.

In the end, therefore, the answer a Christian will give to the question, "Why do you trust the Bible?" is, "Because King Jesus the Resurrected *endorsed* the Old Testament and *authorized* the New." That's not a presupposition. It's not an unthinking,

close-your-eyes-and-jump leap of faith. It's a considered conclusion built from a careful argument that

1. the Bible is historically reliable;
2. Jesus was resurrected from the dead; and
3. the whole of the Bible therefore rests on Jesus's authority.

That's why we believe it.
That's why we trust it.

# A Final Word

# The Next Question

Like I said at the beginning of this book, if you're not a Christian, I truly hope this discussion has challenged you to think about Christians and the Bible in some ways that may differ a bit from how you've thought about them in the past. I hope you've realized that we Christians don't believe what we do without any reasons or simply on the basis of unwarranted presuppositions. I hope you can say now, at least, "Perhaps there's more to the Christian faith than I initially thought."

But I also hope you don't end your exploration of Christianity here. Even if your reading of this book has increased your estimation of the Bible's reliability only *marginally*, I hope you'll take the time to move on to the next and even more important question, the one that the Bible itself holds out repeatedly and preeminently: Who, exactly, is Jesus?

Who did he say he was? And why does it matter? In the end, coming to the conclusion that the *Bible* is reliable is really just a means to another end, the end of coming to know that *Jesus* is reliable. The apostle John, I think, says it best:

these are written so that you may believe
that Jesus is the Christ,
the Son of God,
and that by believing
you may have life in his name.
John 20:31

# Appendix

# Resources for Further Exploration

In this book, I have relied especially on Craig Blomberg's two excellent books, *The Historical Reliability of the Gospels* and *Can We Still Believe the Bible? An Evangelical Engagement with Contemporary Questions*. Both are superb resources for engaging these matters in more depth. In addition, if you'd like to further explore the issues discussed in this book, I recommend beginning with the following helpful resources:

## Bible Translation

Blomberg, Craig L. *Can We Still Believe the Bible? An Evangelical Engagement with Contemporary Questions*. Grand Rapids, MI: Brazos, 2014.

Fee, Gordon D. and Mark L. Strauss. *How to Choose a Bible Translation for All Its Worth: A Guide to Understanding and Using Bible Versions*. Grand Rapids, MI: Zondervan, 2007.

Wegner, Paul D. *The Journey from Texts to Translations: The Origin and Development of the Bible*. Grand Rapids, MI: Baker Academic, 1999.

## Transmission of Biblical Manuscripts

Blomberg, Craig L. *Can We Still Believe the Bible? An Evangelical Engagement with Contemporary Questions*. Grand Rapids, MI: Brazos, 2014.

Metzger, Bruce M. *A Textual Commentary on the Greek New Testament*. 2nd ed. Stuttgart: United Bible Societies, 2012.

Wallace, Daniel B. *Revisiting the Corruption of the New Testament: Manuscript, Patristic, and Apocryphal Evidence*. Grand Rapids, MI: Kregel, 2011.

Wegner, Paul D. *The Journey from Texts to Translations: The Origin and Development of the Bible*. Grand Rapids, MI: Baker Academic, 1999.

## Canonization

Blomberg, Craig L. *Can We Still Believe the Bible? An Evangelical Engagement with Contemporary Questions*. Grand Rapids, MI: Brazos, 2014.

Bruce, F. F. *The Canon of Scripture*. Downers Grove, IL: IVP Academic, 1988.

Hill, C. E. *Who Chose the Gospels? Probing the Great Gospel Conspiracy*. Oxford: Oxford University Press, 2010.

Kruger, Michael J. *Canon Revisited: Establishing the Origins and Authority of the New Testament Books*. Wheaton, IL: Crossway, 2012.

Wegner, Paul D. *The Journey from Texts to Translations: The Origin and Development of the Bible*. Grand Rapids, MI: Baker Academic, 1999.

## The Reliability of Biblical Authors

Blomberg, Craig L. *Can We Still Believe the Bible? An Evangelical Engagement with Contemporary Questions*. Grand Rapids, MI: Brazos, 2014.

————. *The Historical Reliability of the Gospels.* 2nd ed. Downers Grove, IL: IVP Academic, 2007.

Bruce, F. F. *The New Testament Documents: Are They Reliable?* 6th ed. Grand Rapids, MI: Eerdmans / Downers Grove, IL: InterVarsity Press, 2003.

Hoffmeier, James K., and Dennis R. Magary, eds. *Do Historical Matters Matter to Faith?: A Critical Appraisal of Modern and Postmodern Approaches to Scripture.* Wheaton, IL: Crossway, 2012.

## The Miracles of Jesus

Blomberg, Craig L. *Can We Still Believe the Bible? An Evangelical Engagement with Contemporary Questions.* Grand Rapids, MI: Brazos, 2014.

Keener, Craig S. *Miracles: The Credibility of the New Testament Accounts.* Grand Rapids, MI: Baker Academic, 2011.

## The Resurrection of Jesus

Habermas, Gary R., and Michael R. Licona. *The Case for the Resurrection of Jesus.* Grand Rapids, MI: Kregel, 2004.

Strobel, Lee. *The Case for the Resurrection: A First-Century Reporter Investigates the Story of the Cross.* Grand Rapids, MI: Zondervan, 2009.

Wright, N. T. *The Resurrection of the Son of God.* Vol. 3 of *Christian Origins and the Question of God.* Minneapolis: Fortress, 2003.

## Old Testament Issues

Hoffmeier, James K., and Dennis R. Magary, eds. *Do Historical Matters Matter to Faith?: A Critical Appraisal of Modern and Postmodern Approaches to Scripture.* Wheaton, IL: Crossway, 2012.

Longman, Tremper, III, and Raymond B. Dillard. *An Introduction to the Old Testament*. 2nd ed. Grand Rapids, MI: Zondervan, 2006.

Wegner, Paul D. *The Journey from Texts to Translations: The Origin and Development of the Bible*. Grand Rapids, MI: Baker Academic, 1999.

## Inspiration and Inerrancy

DeYoung, Kevin. *Taking God at His Word: Why the Bible Is Knowable, Necessary, and Enough, and What That Means for You and Me*. Wheaton, IL: Crossway, 2014.

Kaiser, Walter C., Jr., Peter H. Davids, F. F. Bruce, and Manfred T. Brauch. *Hard Sayings of the Bible*. Downers Grove, IL: InterVarsity Press, 2010.

MacArthur, John, ed. *The Scripture Cannot Be Broken: Twentieth Century Writings on the Doctrine of Inerrancy*. Wheaton, IL: Crossway, 2015.

Packer, J. I. *"Fundamentalism" and the Word of God: Some Evangelical Principles*. Grand Rapids, MI: Eerdmans, 1958.

Sproul, R. C. *Can I Trust the Bible?* Crucial Questions Series 2. Lake Mary, FL: Reformation Trust, 2009.

# General Index

# Scripture Index

# About the Series

The 9Marks series of books is premised on two basic ideas. First, the local church is far more important to the Christian life than many Christians today perhaps realize. We at 9Marks believe that a healthy Christian is a healthy church member.

Second, local churches grow in life and vitality as they organize their lives around God's Word. God speaks. Churches should listen and follow. It's that simple. When a church listens and follows, it begins to look like the One it is following. It reflects his love and holiness. It displays his glory. A church will look like him as it listens to him.

By this token, the reader might notice that all "9 marks," taken from Mark Dever's book, *Nine Marks of a Healthy Church* (Crossway, 3rd ed., 2013), begin with the Bible:

- expositional preaching;
- biblical theology;
- a biblical understanding of the gospel;
- a biblical understanding of conversion;
- a biblical understanding of evangelism;
- a biblical understanding of church membership;
- a biblical understanding of church discipline;

- a biblical understanding of discipleship and growth; and
- a biblical understanding of church leadership.

More can be said about what churches should do in order to be healthy, such as pray. But these nine practices are the ones that we believe are most often overlooked today (unlike prayer). So our basic message to churches is, don't look to the best business practices or the latest styles; look to God. Start by listening to God's Word again.

Out of this overall project comes the 9Marks series of books. These volumes intend to examine the nine marks more closely and from different angles. Some target pastors. Some target church members. Hopefully all will combine careful biblical examination, theological reflection, cultural consideration, corporate application, and even a bit of individual exhortation. The best Christian books are always both theological and practical.

It's our prayer that God will use this volume and the others to help prepare his bride, the church, with radiance and splendor for the day of his coming.

## Other 9Marks Books

*Church in Hard Places: How the Local Church Brings Life to the Poor and Needy*,
Mez McConnell and Mike McKinley (2016)

*The Compelling Community: Where God's Power Makes a Church Attractive*,
Mark Dever and Jamie Dunlop (2015)

*The Pastor and Counseling: The Basics of Shepherding Members in Need*, Jeremy
Pierre and Deepak Reju (2015)

*Who Is Jesus?*, Greg Gilbert (2015)

*Nine Marks of a Healthy Church*, 3rd edition, Mark Dever (2013)

*Finding Faithful Elders and Deacons*, Thabiti M. Anyabwile (2012)

*Am I Really a Christian?*, Mike McKinley (2011)

*What Is the Gospel?*, Greg Gilbert (2010)

*Biblical Theology in the Life of the Church: A Guide for Ministry*, Michael
Lawrence (2010)

*Church Planting Is for Wimps: How God Uses Messed-up People to Plant Ordinary
Churches That Do Extraordinary Things*, Mike McKinley (2010)

*It Is Well: Expositions on Substitutionary Atonement*, Mark Dever and Michael
Lawrence (2010)

*What Does God Want of Us Anyway? A Quick Overview of the Whole Bible*,
Mark Dever (2010)

*The Church and the Surprising Offense of God's Love: Reintroducing the
Doctrines of Church Membership and Discipline*, Jonathan Leeman (2010)

*What Is a Healthy Church Member?*, Thabiti M. Anyabwile (2008)

*12 Challenges Churches Face*, Mark Dever (2008)

*The Gospel and Personal Evangelism*, Mark Dever (2007)

*What Is a Healthy Church?*, Mark Dever (2007)

## Building Healthy Churches

Edited by Mark Dever and Jonathan Leeman

*Church Discipline: How the Church Protects the Name of Jesus*, Jonathan Leeman
(2012)

*Church Elders: How to Shepherd God's People Like Jesus*, Jeramie Rinne (2014)

*Church Membership: How the World Knows Who Represents Jesus*, Jonathan
Leeman (2012)

*Evangelism: How the Whole Church Speaks of Jesus*, J. Mack Stiles (2014)

*Expositional Preaching: How We Speak God's Word Today*, David R. Helm (2014)

*The Gospel: How the Church Portrays the Beauty of Christ*, Ray Ortlund, (2014)

*Sound Doctrine: How a Church Grows in the Love and Holiness of God*, Bobby
Jamieson (2013)

# IX 9Marks

**Building Healthy Churches**

9Marks exists to equip church leaders with a biblical vision and practical resources for displaying God's glory to the nations through healthy churches.

To that end, we want to see churches characterized by these nine marks of health:

1. Expositional Preaching
2. Gospel Doctrine
3. A Biblical Understanding of Conversion and Evangelism
4. Biblical Church Membership
5. Biblical Church Discipline
6. A Biblical Concern for Discipleship and Growth
7. Biblical Church Leadership
8. A Biblical Understanding of the Practice of Prayer
9. A Biblical Understanding and Practice of Missions

Find all our Crossway titles and other resources at 9Marks.org.

Important Questions. Biblical Answers.

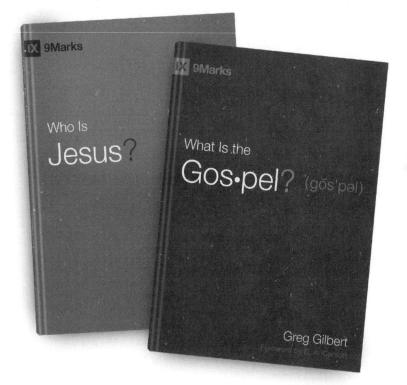